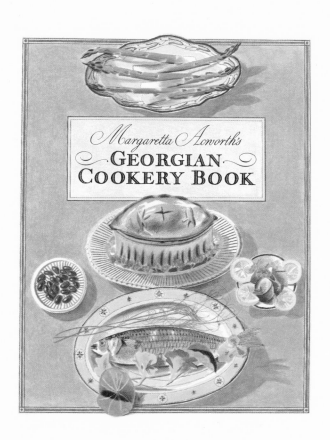

Margaretta Acworth's
GEORGIAN
COOKERY BOOK

Frontispiece from 'The Compleat Housewife' by Eliza Smith, 1727

Margaretta Acworth's GEORGIAN COOKERY BOOK

Edited by Alice and Frank Prochaska

PAVILION
MICHAEL JOSEPH

First published in Great Britain in 1987 by
Pavilion Books Limited
196 Shaftesbury Avenue, London WC2H 8JL
in association with Michael Joseph Limited
27 Wrights Lane, Kensington, London W8 5TZ

Associate editor: Russell Ash
Designed by Bernard Higton

British Library Cataloguing in Publication Data
Acworth, Margaretta
Margaretta Acworth's Georgian cookery book.
1. Cookery, British
I. Title   II. Prochaska, Alice
III. Prochaska, Frank
641.5941   TX717
ISBN 1 85145 124 2 Hdbk
ISBN 1 85145 227 3 Pbk
Printed in Great Britain

TABLE OF CONTENTS

PREFACE

W E came upon the recipe book of Margaretta Acworth when looking for recipes to put into a compendium for the Public Record Office. The compendium never progressed, but Mrs Acworth and her cookery became part of our lives. This edition is based upon a careful trial of her recipes in our own kitchen over a period of several years. To us as historians, not expert cooks, it has been a revelation. We have gleaned new insights into Georgian life by working out the practical implications of these recipes, and we have certainly learned a lot about cooking. Our researches would have been impossible without the rich literature that already exists on traditional English cooking. The doyens of English cookery writers have turned their attention increasingly during the past two decades to the great traditions which still flourished in this country in the eighteenth century, and their works have been our guides. With their help, we have discovered for ourselves the distinguished tradition of English cooking as Mrs Acworth knew it in Georgian London. We hope to pass on some of our own enjoyment to the readers of this book.

The recipes given here are a selection of ninety from about four times that number. A section of medicinal recipes follows the culinary ones in the manuscript, but we have not included these. Mrs Acworth sometimes repeated recipes and often gave several very similar versions of the same dish. A small proportion of her recipes rely on ingredients which cannot now be obtained easily. Some use methods, like elaborate smoking and drying of meats, which can no longer be attempted on a domestic scale. We have excluded repetitious recipes and those which are alien to modern tastes. In making our selection from the remainder, we have tried to keep a balance between the different sorts of food, so that readers will have plenty of choice from which to make their own menus for the modern dinner table. This means that we have included all of Mrs Acworth's few soups but only had room for a proportion of her amazing variety of puddings and cakes. For the same reason, only about half of her recipes for meat and game find a place. We have cooked and eaten all of the recipes given here.

We present the text of Mrs Acworth's original recipes in the form in which they appear in the manuscript. Inconsistent and archaic spellings remain, but we have added punctuation for the sake of clarity. There are few punctuation marks in the original. Often her own instructions are beautifully clear, but there are words and usages which will not be generally familiar. We offer explanations where they seemed necessary, but have tried to avoid the obvious. As far as the interpretation of the recipes is concerned, we have stayed as close as possible to the original. Mrs Acworth often did not give quantities or proportions, so that experimentation was essential, and we have had to rely on our own experience of what worked well and tasted good. Occasionally we have substituted modern versions of ingredients which would have been somewhat different in Mrs Acworth's day. Such deviations are noted in a section at the end of the introduction and individually in the recipes concerned. Sometimes, after trying and enjoying a recipe first in its original form, we have varied it as any cook would do when using her or his own favourite recipes. These changes are not given here; but some readers may feel encouraged to build on Mrs Acworth's legacy of well-tried recipes, with variants of their own.

We are indebted to friends too numerous to name for their readiness to try these dishes at our dinner table, and for much appreciation and encouragement. Some have been kind enough to try out recipes for us in their own kitchens. We would like to thank especially Philippa Dean, Christopher and Jean Elrington and Carole Rawcliffe for their jam-making, wine-making and cake-baking respectively. Helen and Tom Forde supplied us with quinces and Elizabeth and John Oyler loaned us various serving dishes. Our local butcher, Wainwright & Daughter of High Street Kensington, offered sound advice on meat, fish and game. John Jacob, Curator of the Iveagh Bequest, sent notes on the portraits of Margaretta and Abraham Acworth, which hang at Marble Hill House, Twickenham, and are reproduced here. Friends and colleagues at the Public Record Office and Institute of Historical Research have been constant sources of helpful information, and we owe a particular debt to Ann Morton, who first looked at the cookery book of Mrs Acworth. Robert Baldock encouraged us to publish this edition and greatly boosted our morale. Finally, Russell Ash and Marilyn Watts at Pavilion Books have been the most helpful of editors.

London, 1987

INTRODUCTION

MARGARETTA ACWORTH AND HER WORLD

MARGARETTA Acworth's book of recipes has lain tucked away among her family's property deeds since the death of her only surviving son Buckeridge in 1818. He died unmarried and without children, and his estate became the subject of a suit in Chancery after his death. The lawyers took into court as evidence a box of documents which was never reclaimed. It ended up in the Public Record Office among thousands of other unclaimed Chancery Masters' Exhibits. Perhaps a lawyer's clerk sorting quickly through the contents of Buckeridge Acworth's desk failed to notice the vellum-bound volume among the unwieldy parchments. It just got bundled up with the rest of the evidence and taken away. And so a tradition of family cooking and homely medical remedies which had been handed down for at least two generations became hidden from view.

When we found the recipe book and began to experiment with some of the recipes, we did not expect Mrs Acworth to take over our kitchen and our social life as she has done. Her recipes turned out to be easy to interpret and delicious to eat. We enjoyed the freshness of some of the flavours and some unexpected combinations. One day we visited Marble Hill House in Twickenham and found there two recently purchased portraits by the leading court painter Thomas Hudson, of Margaretta Mabella Acworth, née Buckeridge, and her husband Abraham, painted in the year of their marriage, 1745. Each stands in a sylvan setting, Margaretta with a basket of flowers over one arm. Both husband and wife are young and full of life (Margaretta was nineteen, Abraham twenty-six). Abraham's face is full of good nature, well rounded and pink-cheeked above a torso which must have developed into portliness in middle age. Margaretta's portrait, dark, pretty and slender, seems to bespeak a young woman of strong and eager character. We returned to the cookery book, the notes and letters tucked inside it and the legal documents in the box. We discovered a published genealogy of the Acworth family and found some of their wills. The story of Margaretta Acworth's life and the background to her recipes, though tantalizingly incomplete, began to emerge.

Margaretta Acworth, by Thomas Hudson, 1745

Margaretta Acworth was the third child of a Hertfordshire gentleman Anthony Buckeridge and his wife Anne Lewis of Westminster. The family lived in Ware at the time of her birth in 1727 or early 1728. Her father died when she was six or seven and her mother married Edmund Ball, a paymaster of Exchequer bills, four years later. Abraham Acworth, born in 1719, was the son of a Bedfordshire gentleman and his second wife Ann Ball. The genealogy of the family is complicated, but it seems that Margaretta Buckeridge married her stepfather's nephew. At all events, both husband and wife came from prosperous families of the middling gentry, with well-established antecedents in what would now be called the home counties, stretching back to the beginning of the fifteenth century. There were connections on both sides with the Merchant Taylors, and the family had a tradition of sea-faring, although Margaretta's own brother Lewis became an army officer in a regiment of foot. They were founder's kin of St John's College Oxford. They had leasehold tenements in Fleet Street, owned land in Rochester, Kent, which was leased to the Victualling Office, and had some title to lands in Herefordshire. Rather surprisingly for the owners of such extensive property, they apparently did not own a country seat as well, though they may have retreated to rented country houses or stayed with relatives in the summers. The Acworth family had borne arms for at least a century and in 1746, when Margaretta was expecting their first child, Abraham obtained a formal grant of arms for the descendants of his father, John Acworth.

Margaretta and Abraham Acworth were among the more fortunate members of eighteenth-century society when they embarked upon married life. Abraham had recently received a bequest of £30,000 from

Arms of Abraham Acworth, 1748

his uncle Abraham Ball; and Margaretta probably brought with her a substantial dowry from her family in Ware. By her father's will she would inherit an additional £2,000 upon reaching her twenty-first birthday. Abraham had a post as a 'clerk of the Exchequer', which meant that he was in government employment, not necessarily in the Exchequer itself. He may have worked in an office connected with the Navy, for his half-brother Gabriel was a purveyor to the Navy, and an illustrious connection, Sir Jacob Acworth, had been Surveyor of the Navy. His work was suitable for a gentleman but by no means a sinecure. He would have been required to attend daily, except for a recess of about two months in the summer, probably from ten in the morning until four in the afternoon or perhaps for longer. His promotions in government service, recorded in the *Gentleman's Magazine*, suggest that he discharged his duties well.

The couple were married in April 1745 in the Rolls Chapel in Chancery Lane (site now of the Public Record Office where their family records are kept) and settled into the largest house in Smith Street, now Great Smith Street, within sight of Westminster Abbey. This was where Margaretta's mother had grown up. It was on the western edge of the city of Westminster as far as it then extended, close to the Thames and the rural walks of Chelsea. Beyond Chelsea and the village of Kensington, market gardens and nurseries stretched for several miles westwards through Chiswick and out to Twickenham; and from here, as the century progressed, came increasing quantities of fruit and vegetables to feed the swelling population of London. To the east and north of the Acworths' house were all the amenities of city life. Covent Garden and the Haymarket, with their important markets and their great theatres, were barely a mile away. Closer to home were St James's Park, where a large herd of cows grazed, and Green Park, the resort of fashionable promenaders. The government offices in Whitehall and Westminster Hall itself were close enough for Abraham Acworth's work to be only a short stroll from home, and a jumble of ale-houses, coffee-houses and small shops clustered round them.

Smith Street itself had been laid out forty years before. It was named after the owner of the land, Sir James Smith, who later built Smith Square and several of the surrounding streets. By 1745 a small network of streets covered the land between Smith Street and Smith Square, all with rows of elegant, well-built houses of brown brick. The Acworths' house, which unfortunately no longer stands, would have been light and airy, probably four storeys high, well provided with domestic offices, outhouses and stabling, and with quarters for several servants. Its garden probably extended to the back of Dean's Yard and overlooked Westminster School. The street fronted a bowling alley on the western side of

Abraham Acworth, by Thomas Hudson, 1745

Peter Street. Its residents, according to a poll book of 1749, were mostly gentlemen and their households, but they included a blacksmith and a linendraper; and a great array of trades and occupations was represented among the voters living in the immediate neighbourhood. This was the heart of the court area of Westminster, where many of the Acworths' friends and neighbours would have been government office holders and Members of Parliament. There were literary associations too. The essayist Richard Steele had been an early resident and when the Acworths moved in, Thomas Southerne, author of the successful drama *Oroonoko*, was still living in the street.

Abraham Acworth must have been pleased to have literary neighbours, for his will shows that he was himself a reading man and lover of the arts. He bequeathed books, pictures and a collection of prints to his family at his death in 1781. His son Buckeridge, inheritor of his father's library, left sets of the *Tatler*, *Spectator* and *Guardian*, a biographical dictionary, some volumes on India, a universal history, volumes of Shakespeare and a copy of Richardson's *Pamela*, together with a telescope which clearly was also a prized possession. In his will he also left instructions that the portraits of his parents, which now hang in Marble Hill House, be destroyed if they were not wanted, 'for I do not like to have family pictures exposed in a broker's shop'.

The way of life that Abraham and Margaretta Acworth enjoyed would have offered many pleasures beyond those of the table and domestic life. To a young couple of fashion and fortune, London held out almost innumerable possibilities. *The General Advertiser* for early 1745, a newspaper which the couple may have read, gives some of them. *The Provok'd Wife* was playing at Drury Lane with Mr Garrick as Sir John Brute and Mrs Woffington as Lady Brute. At the Theatre Royal Covent Garden, *The Relapse; or Virtue in Danger* was on offer with Mr Cibber as Lord Foppington, and at the King's Theatre Haymarket there was a new musical drama called *Hercules* 'composed by Mr Handel'. Here the pit and boxes were to be put together and tickets sold for half a guinea each, whereas the rival theatres were charging five shillings for a box. There was a drawing of the state lottery, and a party of foot guards was to conduct the lottery wheels back afterwards from the Guildhall to the Lottery Office in Whitehall.

Other attractions included firework displays at Ranelagh Gardens, which were within walking distance of Smith Street. Fireworks were very popular with Londoners. In 1749, Handel performed his Music for the Royal Fireworks in Green Park at a great display to celebrate the signing of the Treaty of Aix-la-Chapelle the year before; and the Duke of Richmond bought up the remaining fireworks to give an even more spectacular display on the Thames. Handel rehearsed his fireworks music in public at Vauxhall Gardens, which were then at the height of their popularity. The Acworths could reach them by taking a boat or the horse ferry across the river from the end of Horseferry Road, also a short walk away, until in 1750 the long-projected Westminster Bridge was opened. For the more serious minded, the *General Advertiser* printed a list of the preachers appointed to preach before the King during the Lent term.

Items of interest in the papers of the day included an advertisement for the Turkey Stone for the teeth, which 'by a few times rubbing to the Teeth, . . . renders them white as Ivory, though ever so black, provided they are not decay'd'. This was for sale in Cornhill near the Royal Exchange and also at a shop on the corner of Pall Mall. Also to be found in Cornhill was a warehouse for morning gowns and 'banjans'. (Presumably these were bandanas intended to complete the informality of a lady's morning toilette.) Elsewhere one might procure a range of medicines which competed with those made at home by Mrs Acworth. It is to be hoped she never needed Dr Hooper's Female Pills, which were 'the best medicine ever discovered for young women, when afflicted with what is vulgarly called, the Green-sickness which two or three Boxes will certainly cure; and are also excellent for the Palpitation of the Heart, Giddiness, Loathing of Food, bad Digestion, Pains of the Stomach, a Beating of the Arteries of the Neck, Short Breath upon every little Motion, sinking of the Spirits, a dejected countenance, and Dislike to Exercise and Conversation, and likewise to the Sulks'.

Intermixed with this miscellany of entertainments and remedies were advertisements for treatises on the defence of England, on exploration and other serious subjects, and for a series of public lectures on chemistry. Given the naval connections in the family and Abraham's employment, the shipping news and military and naval announcements would have aroused the Acworths' interest. It was a period of swiftly moving political events, and the couple lived at the centre of them. The year of their marriage was the year of the great Jacobite rising led by Charles Stuart, the Young Pretender. Bonny Prince Charlie's forces never got near London, but there were Jacobites in the metropolis, and anti-Jacobite scares arose from time to time for years afterwards.

It is extremely unlikely that Abraham Acworth, holding office in government as he did, cherished any Jacobite or Tory sympathies in the 1740s. The poll book of the Westminster by-election in 1749 shows that he voted for the Court candidate against the Independent, who was suspected of Jacobite leanings. A lifelong supporter of the Court party, he would have been shocked by the development of radicalism in London politics, and the Wilkite riots of the 1760s. During Abraham's and Margaretta's married life, the growth of English trade, the defence of the colonies and war with France would have provided constant matter for anxiety and debate. In their middle age, they saw the revolt of the American colonies have profound effects on politics in London and, ultimately, on the whole manner in which national government was carried on. Abraham Acworth did not live quite long enough to play a part in the great administrative reforms carried out in 1782. These effectively created modern government departments and were intended to sweep away the inefficiencies and abuse which had made it impossible to carry on a war against colonists three thousand miles away.

These events were in the distant future when Margaretta Acworth set up house in April 1745, probably with about five or six domestic servants and equipped for most domestic contingencies by her book of 'receipts'. This book, the wills of her husband and son, and a genealogy of the family published in 1910 contain most of the available information about the Acworths. They had three sons, of whom the third, Charles, died in infancy. Their second son Abraham died at the age of twenty-one in 1773. Only Buckeridge Ball Acworth, the eldest, born in 1746, survived his parents. It was he who died without issue in 1818, cherishing, if the genealogist is correct, an unrequited love from his youth. He left much of his estate to the children of his youthful sweetheart and to various societies for promoting Christianity. In 1769 Abraham's half-brother Gabriel died leaving a numerous family, and Abraham seems to have assumed some responsibility for them. A letter of 1778 from a family friend survives among the legal documents, which reports on the continuing delinquency of Abraham's nephew Tom at St John's College, Oxford, and encloses a summary of his debts, including a sum for breakage of glass. Five years later, Tom Acworth died after a fall.

As far as we can judge, Abraham and Margaretta themselves led exemplary lives. They were members of the Church of England, probably devout members, for several of Margaretta's recipes were intended for fasting days, and Abraham's will recorded that he had given generously to Anglican charities in aid of the poor during his life. They baptized their son Abraham at the great new church of St John's Smith Square, which was their parish church. But they may have worshipped regularly at Westminster Abbey, for both of them are buried there in the north cloister. Abraham died at the age of sixty-one, on 4 April 1781, and was buried in the grave of his son Abraham. Margaretta survived for thirteen years. She died on 15 April 1794, aged sixty-seven. They had lived, as far as we can discover, the busy, decent lives of middling gentlefolk in the heart of Westminster, rather more prosperous than many of their class but not, it would seem, pretentious. Philanthropy and an unostentatious devotion to the Church of England characterized the family. It was a life of some personal sorrows, but they were in close touch with numerous friends and relatives, in whom they found support. These few available details are unremarkable enough. It is through her recipes that we know Margaretta Acworth best.

Margaretta Acworth's recipe book was probably written out for her by her mother, Anne Ball. Hers may be the flowing hand in which the tables of contents and the first 128 recipes are set out. Margaretta added continually to the book and exchanged recipes with friends and relatives, often copying them out into the book even though she also kept the original notes and letters. Some of the 350 or so recipes included in the manuscript therefore date from the 1720s or earlier, and may well have been handed down to Mrs Ball by her own mother. The cookery book as a whole was clearly used by Mrs Acworth through her own married life, so it spans at least seventy years of cooking. This is the working cookery book of a practical housewife in affluent circumstances. It is remarkable among other things because it gives us what no published cookery book of the same period could do with such authority, a collection of recipes which we know were used, and used in one particular household. This makes it all the more useful to understand something of the culinary and cultural tradition which formed the background to Mrs Acworth's personal style of cookery and housekeeping.

At the beginning of the century, a strong native tradition of cooking in Britain already relied heavily on foreign imports and a flourishing world-wide trade, using some ingredients, especially spices, citrus fruits, grapes and wine, which had been imported into the country for centuries already. Cooking techniques and the utensils available had developed gradually, and the open fires and ranges, with brick or pottery ovens often alongside them, which were still the best method of cooking available, were not superseded until the 1780s by widespread use of closed ranges resembling the forerunner of a modern kitchen stove. Within these limitations great ingenuity was employed. Already by the end of the seventeenth century, for example, clockwork turnspits were in use, and the range of cooking utensils available proliferated greatly during the century. Ice houses were already in the gardens of people of wealth and fashion by the beginning of the eighteenth century. By 1700 several cookery books had been published, but it was in the Georgian period that the popular market for cookery books really developed. The works of Eliza Smith (1727), Hannah Glasse (1747), and Elizabeth Raffald (1769) alone went through numerous editions.

These books were intended for housewives, housekeepers and cooks. Their success testifies amongst other things to the growth of publishing, to the growing prosperity of the mercantile and farming middle classes, and almost certainly, to an increased personal purchasing power of women. Their contents demonstrate the interest of a very wide social spectrum in this country in the civilized pleasures of eating and drinking. They also include, along with culinary recipes, many medicinal ones, and diagrams on the formal setting of tables and the disposition of dishes within the two main courses of dinner. They show us how varied the diet of eighteenth-century English people was or could be, at least among the upper and middle classes, with a heavy reliance on meat and game, but an increasing variety of fish and vegetable dishes and innumerable, often delicious, recipes for pies, puddings, custards, creams, cakes, biscuits, jams, preserves, and sweetmeats. The staples of the well-to-do cook, and even of her less fortunate sister too, were flour and sugar (in many different degrees of refinement), butter, eggs in superabundance, and stocks, broths and sauces made from chicken, veal, beef and mutton. Among spices and condiments, salt is mentioned rather less often than one might expect, though heavily used in pickling and preserving meat, and mace, nutmeg, cinnamon, cloves, pepper, rose-water and orange flower water were all commonplace. Jelling agents were calves' feet, hartshorn and isinglass. Raising agents were eggs and yeast.

All cookery was highly labour-intensive (one cake might take three hours of beating to bring it to perfection) and involved long, unhealthy hours spent beside coal and charcoal fires. On the other hand, each kitchen was a community, even in an artisan's or tradesman's house,

To make spanish Green Pottadge of Greene or old Pease

Boyle your pease very Well till they Shell them, consisbully Skim of the Shells When your pottadge are throughly boyled take 3 or 4 shallotts or garlick one Onion a Little Mint a Little parsley Shred them altogether and boyle them In halfe a pound of butter then Straine your pottadge through a Cullender Into the Herbs Stir them together and So Serve them up, you May add a little pepper If your pottadge be White With Greene pease putt some whole pepper as Well as Straine Into the broath.

43

To Cellar venison

Take your Venison and bone It then cutt It Inpeices a bove ye breath of your hand If it be Not Hung debone It with ye back of your Cleaver to Make It tender Season It with dried herb Seasoning then put Into your pott one Laying of fatt and an other of Leane If you please you May putt In a Lay of Lard or two press It close In your pott till you thinke It full Enough putt In Good Store of butter putt up your pott Lett It Stand In your oven till It be very tender When you take It out open your pott and pour out your Gravey then Whilst It Is Hott Lay on a Light Weight and press It close then fill It up With Clarifyed butter and If It be Not Hung Soake It In pump Water

44

A page from Mrs Acworth's 'book of receipts'

where the housewife might have had a maid and a couple of daughters to assist her. The community of cooking and eating spread out from the home into the street, the market-place and the bakehouse. Pies and home-made bread were commonly taken to be cooked in the local bakehouse and brought home again ready to eat, though rapidly cooling. Markets for fruit, vegetables, meat and fish were seldom many streets away if you lived in a town. Itinerant tinkers and pedlars carried their wares from house to house, even in the most remote areas, taking with them recipes, news of cooking techniques, cures for everyday ailments, and all sorts of utensils. In large towns and especially in London which was by far the largest city, housekeeping was an even more sociable activity. Costermongers and street vendors plied their wares with familiar street cries, and small street markets were never far away.

The cookery books written by and for eighteenth-century women are revealing cultural documents. More markedly than some of the cookery books by men (which included some by court chefs like Patrick Lamb), the women writers emphasized that they wanted to be practical and down to earth. Hannah Glasse is most famous of them all for her aim to explain cookery in terms that plain cooks and kitchen maids could understand. 'If I have not wrote in the high, polite Stile,' she remarked in

A dinner for a public banquet

The Art of Cookery made Plain and Easy, 'I hope I shall be forgiven; for my Intention is to instruct the lower Sort, and therefore must treat them in their own way.' She was far from being alone in her view that good plain English cooking was to be preferred to French. 'So much is the blind Folly of this Age', she lamented, 'that they would rather be impos'd on by a French Booby, than give Encouragement to a good English cook!'

Many are the complaints in eighteenth-century diaries and memoirs, as well as cookery books, that no good came from aping the French, that plain English ingredients were much better than French ones. This insistence remained strong throughout the century and only began to disappear after the influence of French chefs and restaurateurs became pervasive after the Revolution of 1789. Despite such views, there was no want of attention to presentation in eighteenth-century English cooking. Eliza Smith's *The Compleat Housewife* and Charles Carter's *The Complete Practical Cook* both paid great attention to making dishes look attractive. The setting out of courses, with their side dishes and centrepieces, was a concern to innumerable housewives and not the preserve of grand and formal households only.

Nor is it true that English cooks only learned to cook sauces from the French. English regional cookery is full of sauces and elaborate composite dishes, of which Mrs Acworth gives some excellent examples. The flow of influence between the two countries was to some extent a two-way traffic, at least until the mid-eighteenth century. Yet during the century the balance of culinary fashion and accomplishment did tilt decisively towards the French. One of the most plausible explanations for this, put forward in Stephen Mennell's *All Manners of Food*, is the spread of court influence in France. The French courtiers, for reasons dating back to the personal subservience of the old aristocracy to Louis XIV, attached greater social significance than the English to the precise observance of personal customs and rituals, which included everything to do with food. Great courtiers prided themselves on employing great chefs, who in turn would name their finest sauces and other creations after their patrons. But there was also a strong regional tradition of good cooking in France, which undoubtedly drew strength from the courtly example but cannot wholly be explained by it. It remains a puzzle to account for the decline of an equally strong tradition of good regional cooking in Britain. Both the decline and its causes are to be found in the nineteenth rather than the eighteenth century, and hence beyond the scope of this book.

Mrs Acworth's recipe book partakes of some of the best traditions of English cookery. It shows that like other Georgian housewives she supervised her kitchen closely, for there are comments from time to time on her own tastes and way of doing things. Wealthy housewives in the

Family at breakfast, 1742

nineteenth century were less likely to manage their kitchens so closely, passing on greater responsibility to their servants, which is perhaps one of the reasons why cooking in England deteriorated. There was also perhaps a decline in the traditional view that eating and health were intimately linked. With the rise of proprietary medicines, home remedies such as Mrs Acworth knew fell into disuse. This too may have affected the housewife's attitude to her work and the respect in which she was held.

Mrs Acworth's servants, who had to beat eggs for three hours 'until it be froth', were working for a mistress with high standards who knew how things should be done. She was probably a rewarding mistress to work for, since she could afford the finest ingredients. There was no shortage of wine or brandy, for example, even though the long wars with France during her married life made them sometimes scarce and expensive commodities. Butter, which cost as much as the best meat, was used lavishly. Fine spices, almonds, oranges and lemons were in plentiful supply. Her cookery was traditional and thoroughly English. Relatively few French terms appear in the recipes, beyond those universally in use, such as 'ragout' or 'fricacy'. At a time when English cookery still varied greatly between regions, Margaretta Acworth's cooking was based on that of London and south-eastern England, although some of her relatives may have supplied recipes from the West Country. It is also likely that she was familiar with some of the published cookery books of the day. She used in her own cookery book, with a few minor changes, about a dozen recipes which also appear in Eliza Smith's *The Compleat Housewife*.

The quantities were often large, suggesting either that the household was large or that the Acworths entertained on a huge scale. Eggs were used unsparingly and it is not uncommon to find recipes that call for twelve, eighteen or even twenty-two of them. Suet was a popular ingredient and must have produced rather greasy pies and puddings. But, interestingly, several of the recipes for soups and sauces specify that the fat must be skimmed off before they are used. There is a notable absence of recipes for fresh vegetables. We have assumed that they were used, but almost always simply boiled or, in the case of salads, raw. There is no way of telling whether she overcooked them in too much water, an error which writers as different as Hannah Glasse and Arthur Young both warned against. Mrs Acworth mentions fresh vegetables just often enough to show that she cooked a good variety of them. A dish of veal fricandos was to be served on a bed of sorrel and a pudding called a Fancy was made with spinach juice. Artichoke bottoms appear in a pie in their own right and more than once as part of the garnish for a dish of veal. There is abundant use of mushrooms, morels and truffles. Pickled vegetables there are in plenty, including beans, red cabbage, cucumbers, onions and purslane.

She makes constant use of herbs. 'Sweet herbs', which included basil, marjoram, rosemary and thyme, are seldom absent from any savoury dish. Of them all, parsley was her favourite. Bay leaves and coriander put in an appearance from time to time, though the coriander always appears in sweet recipes. 'Pot herbs', that is onions or shallots, turnips, carrots and celery, were added to stocks. There is an occasional whiff of garlic. Fruits and nuts are used frequently. Jams, jellies and preserves include some delectable recipes for oranges, quinces, plums, grapes, apricots and raspberries. The range of apple recipes is particularly impressive. Dried and candied fruits, especially currants, raisins and citron peel, she used in large quantities.

Some of the recipes in Mrs Acworth's book appear to be of some antiquity. Musk as a flavouring for sweet dishes was supposed to be going out of fashion by the end of the seventeenth century, but the instruction to use 'a grain of Musk' appears quite often here. Similarly with ambergrease. There are other ingredients, foreign to us or used very sparingly now, which were commonplace to Mrs Acworth and typical of the cookery of her day. She used cloves quite often in both sweet and savoury dishes. Mace and nutmeg were also used lavishly as both sweet and savoury seasonings, with mace sometimes substituting for pepper. In one recipe for either pigeons or chickens for example, mace is recommended for the chickens but pepper for the pigeons. Caraway seeds must have been bought in bulk. They dominate several biscuit and cake recipes, either straight or in the shape of 'comfits', which meant that they had been coated in boiling white sugar.

Though there are several recipes for sweetbreads in composite meat dishes and tongue is dished up in various ways, offal was sparingly used. Liver appears only once, when the liver of a hare cooked in milk and cream is used to thicken its sauce. We have found no mention of kidneys, though cocks' combs were quite commonly used, but they do not seem to add very much to a dish apart from colour. Typical of eighteenth-century cooking, venison and game are represented but not here in great profusion. The dominant meat in her cookery was veal, although recipes for mutton and beef are present, and chickens were eaten a lot, never roasted over the fire but stewed, pot-roasted, cooked in a pie or served up with a fricassee. Fish included herrings, anchovies used often as a seasoning, eels, soles, cod, crabs, lobsters, oysters and shrimps and, that favourite from the fishponds of gentlemen's estates, carp.

One could extend indefinitely the catalogue of delicacies consumed by the Acworth household. They had access both to old and to newly fashionable ingredients. Sea fish, for example, were beginning to be more widely consumed in England as a whole, thanks to improved methods of transport which could bring them fresh inland. Mrs Acworth was quite accustomed to using them from her privileged position within easy reach of Billingsgate, the great fish market served by the Thames and its nearby sea ports. But she also had a recipe for pickling herrings by the hundred in barrels, which must have derived from earlier times. In her use of sugar she shows a fine disregard for cost, frequently specifying the most expensive 'double refined' sugar which would have been close in texture to modern caster sugar. Here too she was in the new fashion. The English became famous in the eighteenth century for their consumption of sugar, and have never lost the reputation since.

It is characteristic of Georgian cooking to find sweet and savoury recipes mixed together, meat in a sweet pie, potted meat served with sugar, and so on. Mrs Acworth is no exception in this respect. She was also a woman of her time in the attention she paid to the appearance of her food. Buttered crabs or lobsters were to be prepared in their shells with little triangles of toast; forcemeat balls embellished several recipes for chicken or fowl; she had seen one clear soup served up with a toast floating in it; a veal dish was to be garnished with slices of orange and fried parsley; cakes were often iced; and she left tucked in between the pages of her book three small cut-outs of parchment in the shape of flowers and thistles.

What we cannot tell from her manuscript is precisely which dishes she served together, and when and how the Acworths sat down to table. If they were typical of households in the metropolis, they probably breakfasted lightly on a spiced roll such as a wig or possibly a piece of cake, taken with tea, coffee or hot chocolate. Margaretta may have taken up the fashion of serving afternoon tea with cakes and sweetmeats. In the evening, perhaps at about six o'clock, she and Abraham would have eaten dinner, the one big meal of the day. In the presence of guests, this would have consisted of two courses. Each course consisted of at least two or three main dishes and several side dishes laid out on the table in symmetrical patterns. The first course would have been the heavier of the two, including fish, meat and game, sauces, vegetables served usually as a garnish, and perhaps a sweet pudding. If soup was on the menu it would have been eaten first and replaced with a fish dish. The second course also included meat and fish but with these savouries there would have been a greater variety of puddings, creams or tarts. The diners were not expected to sample every dish but would have taken small portions of whatever took their fancy. If a dessert was served, it was a feast for the eyes as well as the palate, with fruits, jellies, marmalades and other sweetmeats attractively set out in a variety of little dishes and in pyramids on raised dishes. After dessert and perhaps a glass of wine, the ladies would have retired.

A cookery book published in 1758, the *Art of Cookery* by Alice Smith, gives a helpful glimpse of the English hostess at work. To her we may turn for a likely description of how Margaretta Acworth presented the handiwork of her kitchen: 'At present the fashion is, after the lady at the head of the table has made a beginning, by helping those near her, for every one to take care of himself, by helping himself to what is next, or sending his plate to the person who sits near what he likes; so that the lady fares like the rest of the company, and has no more trouble than others. This is civility to her, because it excuses her a great deal of trouble, without taking from her the opportunity of serving her friends.' She goes on to remark that 'In the old times in England, people thought they never entertained one another well, if they did not fed them 'till they almost burst; . . . but this is a custom set aside for a much more reasonable civility.' The guests at Margaretta Acworth's table may not have burst, but they certainly did not waste away. For the character that shines through her recipe book is of a generous and graceful spirit, who liked to do things well.

A Note on Quantities and Modern Ingredients

LIKE most housewives and cooks of her day, Mrs Acworth rarely gave exact measurements for all the ingredients in her recipes. Still less was she able to give precise instructions for the heat at which any given recipe should be cooked, since thermometers were not available for domestic use, and the heat of ovens could not be regulated at the touch of a button or the turn of a knob. Her instructions were often precise in her own terms (e.g. to cook certain recipes in the oven when it was cooking brown bread, or to use eight large or nine small eggs, leaving out half the whites). To use her recipes is to admire time and again the manual dexterity, the patience, the skilled judgement that made cooking in an eighteenth-century kitchen a craft of a high order. Mrs Acworth's skills also remind the cook in the late twentieth century (if reminder be needed) that cookery is anything but an exact science.

It follows that any quantities given for our modern versions of Mrs Acworth's recipes are liable to be subjective and inexact. We have given measurements as carefully as possible first in British imperial or avoirdupois measures, then in grams or millilitres rounded to a convenient figure, and then in American cup and spoon measurements where appropriate. Where only cups and spoons are mentioned (e.g. for quantities too small to be measured by the average kitchen scales), it is the US standard ones that have been used. In some recipes we give an indication of the number of servings they will produce, but since the appetites of families and friends are as infinitely variable as the judgement of cooks themselves, we have made no attempt to be thorough in this respect. How many biscuits in a batch? What size of cake will feed an average household? And how many servings in a pint of soup? At the Acworths' table, probably laden with several main and side dishes to each course, the answers to these questions would have been quite different from our own.

The measures used in eighteenth-century England were not all the same as those used now. Some (e.g. the 16 oz pint) are still in use in America though they were ousted here in the late nineteenth century by imperial measures. Metric measures have been taking over patchily, supported by the endeavours of the Metrication Board, but will still be more familiar to the continental European than to the British cook. The table below is designed to show the main measures used by Mrs Acworth, with their modern imperial, metric and American equivalents.

TABLE OF SOLID AND LIQUID MEASURES

18th-century English	Imperial 20th-century British	Metric	US to nearest part of a cup
1 oz	1 oz	30 g/ml	1 tbsp flour
2 oz	2 oz	60 g/ml	⅓ cup flour ¼ cup liquid
4 oz, ¼ lb, ¼ pint	4 oz, ¼ lb	115 g/ml	¾ cup flour ½ cup liquid
5 oz	5 oz	150 g/ml	1 cup flour
6 oz	6 oz	170 g/ml	1¼ cups flour ¾ cup liquid
8 oz, ½ lb, ½ pint	8 oz, ½ lb	225 g/ml	1⅔ cups flour 1 cup liquid
10 oz	10 oz, ½ pint	280 g/ml	2 cups flour 1¼ cups liquid
16 oz, 1 lb, 1 pint	16 oz, 1 lb	450 g/ml	3 cups + 1 tbsp flour 2 cups liquid 1 US pint
20 oz	20 oz, 1 pint	560 g/ml	4 cups flour

A second problem in adapting old recipes for modern use is finding the right ingredients. In the case of Mrs Acworth's cookery this is not so difficult as some might suppose, for the great majority of her ingredients are familiar to the modern cook. A few of those she used regularly are now rarities but still obtainable; and a tiny proportion simply cannot be obtained in a form suitable for culinary use. Some of the most familiar foods appear in strange forms, and these too call for some explanation. Since our concern in preparing this edition has been to provide practical versions for modern life, we have used nothing that was not obtainable in our own normal shopping round. Readers more persistent than ourselves may well be able to find the originals in a few cases where we have used substitutes. The following list contains a selection of ingredients with a note of how we have coped with them. Others which appear in particular recipes are explained where they arise.

Almonds Usually ground in Mrs Acworth's recipes using rose-water or orange flower water to prevent oiling. We use commercially ground almonds with a little almond essence to return the flavour which the processing removes.

Butter The finest butter was said to come from Suffolk, but the most important thing was that it should be fresh. We have suggested using a combination of butter and soft margarine, or substituting margarine altogether in some recipes, but in other cases the flavour and texture of the full quantity of butter are clearly essential to the recipe.

Citron A fruit similar to lemon, invariably used here for its candied peel. It can be obtained in chunks, but we have used the universally obtainable mixed chopped peel instead.

Eggs There is no reason to suppose that the eggs Mrs Acworth used were significantly smaller than modern ones, although their size would have been more erratic, adding to the imprecision of the quantities she gives. We have used modern European size 4 eggs, which are slightly smaller than average.

Flour Mrs Acworth's flour would have been stone-ground and unbleached, but in most cases probably the whitest she could procure. Except where otherwise specified, we have used 'wheatmeal', or 85 per cent extraction flour. It is largely a matter of taste, but lighter flours may produce slightly different results from ours. Self-raising flour and baking powder were not available and we have not used them.

Mace and Nutmeg Mrs Acworth used blades of mace and whole nutmegs. We have found it most convenient to use ground mace all the time and to grind our own nutmegs most of the time, occasionally resorting to ready-ground nutmeg.

Musk This powerful scent obtained from the glands of the male musk deer appears in Mrs Acworth's plum jelly and a few other recipes as an optional ingredient. We have disregarded it.

Orange flower water This can be obtained from chemists and some supermarkets or specialist grocery stores. We have used essence of orange flower water, and only in tiny quantities, because it is very powerful.

Palates The roof of the mouth of an ox. Mrs Acworth used these in small slices as a garnish in several recipes. We have substituted tongue, or omitted them altogether.

Rose-water This too can be obtained from chemists, but it is not difficult to find in grocery stores owned by Cypriot, Greek or Middle Eastern proprietors, and is in many supermarkets. The version we have found is not so potent as the essence of orange flower water, though still to be used sparingly.

Sack A generic name for a class of white wines imported from Spain and the Canaries, essentially the forerunner of montilla and sherry. We use dry sherry.

Salt The common kitchen salt which Mrs Acworth would have used most of the time would have been rock salt from Cheshire, sold in blocks. Occasionally she specifies bay salt for her more exacting pickle recipes, and this would probably have been specially refined sea salt from Portugal. If she was being inexact, she may have meant sea salt from Maldon in Essex, which was held by Hannah Glasse to be very good. We use sea salt wherever salt is specified.

Sweet Herbs Mrs Acworth generally spelled them 'yerbs'. She meant the equivalent of a modern bouquet garni, and we have taken this to include basil, a bay leaf, marjoram, parsley, rosemary and thyme (all of which she named) or whatever other non-bitter herb was to hand.

Suet Mrs Acworth used both beef and veal suet (kidney fat), which she generally shredded finely. Modern shredded beef suet in a packet is a perfectly acceptable version. We have adopted the habit, however, of substituting freshly grated breadcrumbs for all or part of the suet in her recipes. The lavish use of suet in eighteenth-century kitchens made for some rather greasy cookery which most people today would not find to their taste.

Sugar The sugar imported from the West Indian colonies and elsewhere was refined in England to varying degrees of whiteness, the finest and whitest being the most expensive. Mrs Acworth probably bought coarse, whitish sugar by the loaf for everyday use. She often used double-refined sugar, and occasionally beat this to a powder, e.g. for icing. Very occasionally she specified Lisbon sugar, which was a fine brown sugar imported via Portugal; and for preserves she probably used preserving sugar in coarse crystals. Where not otherwise specified, we have used granulated sugar. Caster sugar is the best modern version of 'double-refined', and icing sugar can be used in recipes which call for the sugar to be beaten very fine.

Yeast Eighteenth-century cooks generally used ale yeast, which could be purchased from a brewery. It imparted a distinctly beery flavour to breads and cakes if it was not washed well before use. Modern dried yeast is the easiest substitute to use, though we may thereby reduce the liquid content of some recipes a little.

CHAPTER ONE

SOUPS AND

POTTAGES

White Soup
Strong Broth
Gravy Soup
A Very Good Pottage
Pease Pottage
Spanish Green Pottage
Mock Turtle

Spanish Green Pottage

POTTAGES of the medieval and early modern period had been substantial, nourishing meals in themselves. Made with all sorts of grains, pulses, pot herbs and meats, they were cooked for a long time so that the meat and cereals turned to a mush that could be eaten with a spoon. They continued to be standard fare for a large part of the British population throughout the eighteenth century. The very poor subsisted mainly on a diet of bread and cheese varied by pottages which often contained little or no meat. For members of the middling and upper classes, soups began to take over from pottages, especially after forks came into widespread use in the second half of the seventeenth century.

The soups of Mrs Acworth's circle were usually meat broths served with sweet herbs such as parsley and pot herbs like celery, onion and lettuce sliced into them, and commonly with a piece of toasted manchet or French bread or a roll floating in the middle. Often they would be served with some of the meat in the middle or sliced into the soup. Their place in the meal was as part of the first course, but typically they would be set at the top of the table and offered first, then removed and replaced with a dish of fish. In this custom lay the beginnings of the modern ordering of courses at a full-scale dinner, where soup is followed by fish, then by a meat dish with vegetables and finally by desserts, cheeses and fruit. The eighteenth-century way of doing it must have meant that the soup and the fish would be eaten hot, while the other dishes cooled before the eyes of the diners. Any other dish which the hostess wished to serve hot from the kitchen would have been brought in as a 'remove' after the soup.

Mrs Acworth did not have many recipes for soups. Those she had were probably made to do double duty as basic broths and stocks for use in her numerous sauces. Her way of serving soups is a good illustration of the changes that were taking place in English cooking, for in more than one recipe she leaves open the option of serving the meat or a fowl and Forcemeat balls in the soup. There is an echo of earlier customs too in the almonds which go into the excellent White Soup. Almonds had been a basic ingredient of many medieval pottages, including the forerunners of Blancmange (see p. 122). The pottage recipes hark back to an earlier tradition, and were probably served as side dishes which would have remained on the table throughout the first course. None of the recipes is extravagant by the standards of her day. Even the recipe for Mock Turtle (see p. 37), a delicious consommé redolent of cayenne and madeira, is an economical version of the contemporary rage for real turtle soups and dinners in fashionable circles.

TO MAKE A WHITE SUPE Take a Nuckell of Veale and boyle ye broath to jelly and straine it and when cold take of all ye fatt and then put in two Chickings just to boyle, and when they are enough beate ¹/₂ a pound of almonds with a little Creame (to keep it from oyling) and thickning your broath up with it put a blade of mace. In boyling the jelly broath, cut some Chickings or Patridges in peices into ye broath with a little Salt.

WHITE SOUP

THE presence of ground almonds in this soup would have been a commonplace in Georgian cooking. Almonds had been used widely in the kitchens of the wealthy since their introduction to England from the Middle East during the Crusades. At a time when sweet and savoury ingredients were not separated in English cooking, almonds were not identified as specifically belonging among sweet ingredients, and this soup is in fact thoroughly savoury. Served as a soup, it has a delicious flavour and texture. Served with its meats chopped up and replaced in it, it makes an equally good main course.

about 1 lb (450 g) knuckle of veal,
or two large pieces cut for 'osso buco'
2 carrots
1 onion
2 bunches of herbs including bay leaf, marjoram and parsley
salt and pepper
2 pints (1.15 litres, 2½ US pints) water
1 small chicken
1 tablespoon olive oil to brown the chicken
additional salt, pepper and parsley
2 oz (60 g, ⅔ cup) ground almonds
5 fl oz (140 ml, ⅔ cup) thin or thick cream
1 teaspoon ground mace

Place the veal, carrots, onion, herbs and seasoning in a saucepan with the water and bring gently to the boil. Skim, and leave to simmer until the veal is very tender (about 1½ hours). Remove the veal (which you can use for some other dish). Leave the liquid to get completely cold, and scrape the fat off the top. Brown the chicken in a frying pan, put it in the veal stock with a little extra salt and pepper and a fresh bunch of herbs, bring to the boil and then let it simmer gently for about an hour, until the chicken is cooked. Remove the chicken and leave the stock to cool a second time, then skim off the chicken fat. When you are ready to cook the soup finally, mix the ground almonds, mace and cream in a bowl, then add enough of the stock to make a thin paste. Pour the paste into the stock over a gentle heat, whisking well with a wire whisk. Let the soup heat slowly to near boiling point. It can be left indefinitely over a low heat but should not be allowed to boil fiercely. Serve it garnished with thin slivers of chicken breast and some chopped parsley, or as a main course with the veal and chicken chopped up and replaced in it, accompanied by French bread and a salad.

To MAKE STRONG BROTH Take 12 quarts of Water, 3 knuckles of Veal, one hough of Beef, 2 pair of Calves feet, Chickings and Rabits, a Faggot of sweete Yearbys, 2 Onions, a little Mace and pepper, some Lemon Peal. Boyle these tell it comes to six Quarts, then strane it into a Earthen pott.

STRONG BROTH

HERE is a version of the basic all-purpose broth which would have been kept as a foundation for sauces (e.g. in the Ragout of Veal, p. 62) or for serving as a soup at dinner or as a restorative for the sick. It makes a tasty soup in its own right, served with a little rice or vermicelli cooked in it and then sprinkled with chopped parsley. We have substituted a pig's trotter for the calves' feet, which would not fit into most modern saucepans even if you could get hold of them.

4 oz (115 g) each of stewing beef, diced shoulder or breast of veal,
rabbit and chicken cut into pieces (2 small legs of rabbit and a good-
sized chicken thigh will come to about the right weight each)
1 pig's trotter
1 onion
a bunch of parsley, basil and bay leaf
thinly pared zest of $\frac{1}{2}$ lemon
1 teaspoon each of salt, ground mace and pepper
$4\frac{3}{4}$ pints (2.7 litres, 6 US pints) water

Place all the ingredients in a large saucepan and bring to the boil. Leave it to simmer over a moderate heat, covered with a well-fitting lid and gently bubbling, for about 4 hours. By that time the liquid should have reduced to approximately half of its original quantity and will have a good flavour. Strain the broth through a fine sieve and leave it to cool. It will set to a jelly and will keep well for a week in the refrigerator. It can also be frozen. Skim off the fat before using it. The meats can be used in a pie or to make a risotto.

A GRAVY SOUP Gitt a shin of beef, put it in a Small pot of water. Let it be scum'd very Cleane. Put in an Onyon with Glaves, a faggot of hearbs with a small sprig of sweet Basil, some Carrot & Turnips. Fry the Hearbs in a little Butter then putt them in the Soup. Lettice cut gross, sellery & Charvil. The stock must be boyld to a strong Jelly. Splitt Green peas for Pea soup.

GRAVY SOUP

Mrs Acworth tucked this recipe from her cousin Rachel Manaton into her book and later copied it out as well. The mysterious 'glaves' were her rendering of cloves. This recipe makes a tasty basic soup, very good on its own or served with cooked split peas stirred into it, as suggested here. Like the Strong Broth, it also makes a good base for sauces, and can be stored in the refrigerator for a week, or frozen.

about 1 lb (450 g) stewing beef
1 beef leg bone
water to cover (about 2 pints, 1.15 litres, 2½ US pints)
6 cloves
1 medium-sized onion
1 large or 2 small turnips
3 carrots
a large bunch of parsley
3 bay leaves
1 stalk fresh basil (or 1 teaspoon dried)
1 stalk fresh chervil (or about ½ teaspoon dried)
2 sticks celery
1 small round lettuce
1 tablespoon butter
1 tablespoon salt and a little pepper

Place the beef and bone, chopped into a manageable size, in a close-fitting saucepan and cover with water. Bring it quickly to the boil and skim. Stick the cloves into the onion, cut the turnips and carrots into several pieces, and put these into the saucepan with the parsley and bay leaves. Bring it all to the boil, then reduce the heat and leave it to simmer for 2 hours. When the contents of the saucepan are quite cold, strain the liquid into a bowl and leave it in the refrigerator until you are ready to use it. Then chop the remaining herbs finely, and cut the celery and lettuce into thin strips. Melt the butter in a deep saucepan until it froths, fry the herbs, lettuce and celery in it for about 2 minutes, and add the stock. Bring it all to the boil, season with salt and pepper, and serve. The basic recipe can be made into pea soup by blending in a cupful of dried split peas which have been soaked overnight and then boiled briskly in salted water for 40 minutes.

TO MAKE A VERY GOOD POTTADGE To a Knuckle of veal take 3 pound of neck Beefe and 4 palletts. Put all into 3 Gallons of Water. Simer and boyle them easilly 6 or 7 hours till ye Meate is Mash and the palletts tender. Then save ye palletts and straine ye broath, which will jelly. Ye next Day add formickille to your Melted Broath, about 4 spoonfulls brooke small. Then put in with yt 4 Dozen of Cocks Combs scalded and pilled and boyle it till both be tender. Then Having in Readiness Sweete breads fry'd and cutt into Dice, your Palletts must be cut into thin pieces and 3 or 4 blades of mace, 1/2 a quarter of a handfull of Sweete Herbs tyed in a Bunch, put all in together. Simmer them 1/2 an Hour. Soo with a tost of White bread serve it up. Ye Combs may be cutt in bitts too if their large. You may add balls of fforest meate and lay any ffoule in ye Middle of ye Dish tho tis as well without.

A VERY GOOD POTTAGE

THE particularly eccentric spelling of this recipe obscures some simple ingredients: 'formickille' were vermicelli, widely used in clear meat soups; and 'fforest meat' is simply forcemeat. The 'palletts' were beef palates, which are not readily available now. They are gelatinous and similar to tripe when cooked. We have substituted lambs' tongues, with pieces of bacon in place of the similarly unobtainable cocks' combs. This soup is not complicated to make, and has a good meaty flavour.

12 oz (340 g) knuckle of veal
12 oz (340 g) lambs' tongues
1 lb (450 g) stewing beef
10½ pints (4.75 litres, 8 US pints) water
6 oz (225 g) sweetbreads
about 4 oz (115 g) vermicelli
a bunch of herbs including bay leaf, parsley and thyme
salt and pepper to taste
4 slices of bacon
2 slices of bread
a little oil for frying

Cover the veal, tongues and beef with water in a large saucepan, bring them to the boil and then simmer until the tongues are tender and the beef and veal falling apart (up to 6 hours). Strain the broth and trim the skin and gristle off the tongues, and keep them in the refrigerator. Next day, prepare the sweetbreads by soaking them for 2 hours in cold water with a dash of lemon juice or vinegar, then scalding them for 2 minutes in hot water, and removing the membranes. Slice them thinly and fry for about 5 minutes until they are tender. Heat the broth and add the sweetbreads, vermicelli broken into short lengths, the tongues cut into thin strips and the herbs, salt and pepper. Simmer gently for about 20 minutes. Meanwhile fry the bacon and bread, cut up into small dice, until both are crisp. Add some to each portion of the soup as you serve it.

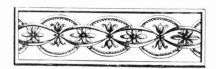

TO MAKE PEASE POTTAGE Take a peck of pease shelled and Washed. Put them into a stew pann with three leaved Lettice, a little parsley, a little pursline, pepper and salt. Take ½ a pound of butter. Mingle them altogether and set them on Coales and let them stew till they be Enough.

PEASE POTTAGE

THIS is an excellent way of cooking fresh, young peas. Jane Grigson includes a modern French recipe using peas and purslane in her *Vegetable Book*, so the combination has stood the test of time. Mrs Acworth would probably have served this pottage as a side dish with the first course. For modern dinners, it serves equally well as a simple starter or as an accompaniment to meat or fish. Purslane, unfortunately, is difficult to obtain unless you grow the plants yourself. In its absence, double the quantity of parsley.

about 1½ lbs (675 g) fresh peas, which will come to 1 lb (450 g)
when shelled
the inner leaves of a small round lettuce
1 oz (30 g) each fresh parsley and purslane, or 2 oz (60 g) parsley
salt and pepper to taste
2 oz (60 g, ¼ cup) butter

Shell the peas. Chop the lettuce leaves coarsely and put them in the bottom of a saucepan. Chop the parsley and purslane finely and add that and the peas, salt and pepper. Cut the butter into small dice and strew it on top. Cover the pan and leave it over a moderate heat, stirring occasionally, until the peas are cooked (about 20 minutes). This pottage should be served as soon as possible after it is cooked, and should be stirred only enough to keep it from sticking to the pan, so that the fresh, juicy texture of the peas is preserved.

To MAKE SPANISH GREEN POTTADGE OF GREEN OR OLD PEESE Boyle your peese very well till they shell then constantly skim of the Shells. When your pottadge are thoroughly boyled take 3 or 4 shallots or garlicke, one Onion, a little Minte, a little parsley, shred them altogether and boyle them in half a pound of butter then Straine your pottadge through a cullender into the Herbs. Stir them together and so serve them up. You may add a little pepper. If your pottadge be Maide with Green peese put some whole pepper as well as Straine into the broath.

SPANISH GREEN POTTAGE

THIS soup has a delicate flavour. Using the proportions given here, it is not thick like some better-known versions of pea soup, but a sediment of peas tends to sink to the bottom while the herbs and butter rise to the top; so it is advisable to stir with the ladle once or twice while you are serving it. Croûtons of white bread fried in a mixture of butter and olive oil make a good addition. The quantities given here serve six people amply.

8 oz (225 g, 1 cup) dried peas
about 2½ pints (1.25 litres, 3 US pints) water
1 medium-sized onion
3 or 4 shallots, or 1 clove of garlic
1 cup chopped parsley
½ cup chopped mint
2 oz (60 g, ¼ cup) butter
salt and pepper to taste
parsley, mint and croûtons to garnish

Soak the peas overnight in the water and then bring them to the boil in the same water, skimming the surface well. Cook them briskly for at least 20 minutes until they are soft. Blend the peas in their liquid (or pass them through a sieve), season with a little salt and pepper, and set them to one side. Heat the butter in a large pan over a moderate heat until it froths and stir in the finely chopped onion, shallots or garlic, parsley and mint. When the onions are golden and soft, pour in the peas, stir well, heat gently to near boiling point and taste for seasoning, adding some coarsely ground black pepper if necessary. You may like to add some extra, freshly chopped parsley and mint and croûtons of fried bread as you serve the soup.

*T*O *MAKE ENGLISH TURTLE Take a Calves Head Scald & boyle it. Take the bones out and Cutt it in pieces. Season it with Cuian & Salt to your Tast. Putt it in a Dish or any other Thing you please & putt to it Good Mutton Gravey made pretty Thick and a pint of Madera Wine, some Shread Lemmon peal & some parsley. Ad to it 2 or 3 ox pallats. They are Like Tripe, They Must be Cutt.*

MOCK TURTLE

MOCK turtle appeared soon after green turtles began to be imported from the West Indies for the delectation of wealthy diners. Before long many mock turtle recipes mocked even this one for the meat disappeared altogether. Hence, perhaps, the mournfulness of Lewis Carroll's Mock Turtle, discovered by Alice 'sitting sad and lonely on a little ledge of rock' and uttering that most poignant of elegies to a soup:

Beautiful Soup, so rich and green,
Waiting in a hot tureen!
Who for such dainties would not stoop?
Soup of the evening, beautiful Soup!

Mutton stock made with about 2 lbs (900 g) mutton or lamb on the
bone, 1 carrot, 1 onion, 3 bay leaves, parsley
the meat from a boned calf's head
(or 2 lbs (900 g) of veal knuckle)
½ teaspoon cayenne and salt to taste
juice and rind of 1 lemon
bunch of parsley, 1 carrot and 1 onion
2 egg whites
8 fl oz (225 ml, 1 cup) Madeira or dry sherry
chopped parsley, coarsely grated lemon zest
and croûtons to garnish

To make the mutton stock, cover all the ingredients with water, bring to the boil, then simmer for about 2 hours. Strain the stock and skim off the fat. Place in a large saucepan the calf's head or veal, seasoning, lemon juice and rind, parsley, carrot and onion. Cover them with cold mutton stock, bring to the boil, cover and simmer for 2 to 3 hours. Strain the stock. Trim and dice the gelatinous meat of the calf's head and set it to one side. Replace the stock in the saucepan, whisk in the egg whites, bring it to the boil and let it bubble until the egg whites form a thick scum. Line a sieve with a thin cloth, strain the stock through it into a bowl and return it to the saucepan. Add the Madeira, diced meat, some chopped parsley and grated lemon zest, and bring to the boil. Serve it piping hot, with croûtons.

CHAPTER TWO

FISH AND
FOWL

Cod in Shrimp Sauce
Baked Soles
Carp or Eels in Wine Sauce
Fish Sauce
Buttered Crabs or Lobsters
Grand Roast Turkey
Pot-roasted Chicken or Guinea Fowl
White Fricassee
Fricassee of Chicken or Rabbit
Stewed Chicken with Wine Sauce
Chicken Pie

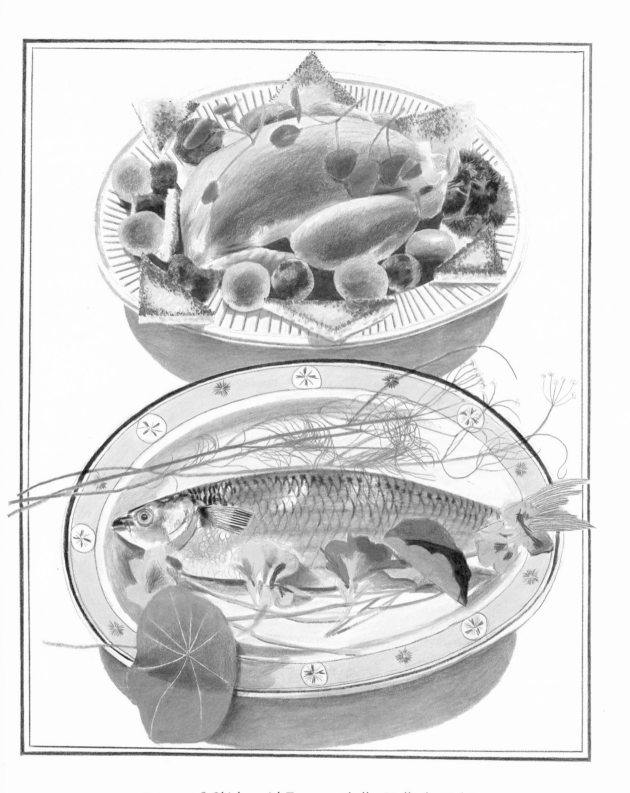

Pot-roasted Chicken with Forcemeat balls; Mullet for Fish Sauce

HE great fish market at Billingsgate opened in 1699, providing Londoners of all classes with plentiful supplies of fish. Throughout the city costermongers trundled cartloads of fish for local sale, and during the eighteenth century a new fish market opened in Broadway, only a short walk from Smith Street. The fish was not always fresh, for some of it travelled slowly to London by road or canal while other varieties were brought to the mouth of the Thames from the fishing ports of Norfolk, Suffolk and Essex in small coastal vessels and then shipped into the city in barges. Ice was not used for transporting fish on a large scale until the end of the century. Published cookery books often included instructions for judging the freshness of sea fish. Although improved methods of transport were gradually making fresh sea fish easier to obtain, fresh-water fish like carp were still very popular. Oysters were cheap and abundant, partly because like some other shellfish, they could be kept alive in brackish water until they were to be eaten.

Mrs Acworth had a variety of recipes for fish and shellfish. Some of them drown the flavour of the fish itself in heavy spices and ale or wine. Presumably this was a deliberate defence against tainted fish. In the recipes included here, the balance of flavours is more delicate. The Buttered Crab and Lobster, which we find delicious starters, were often recommended as second-course dishes in published cookery books. Most of the others would have been served by Mrs Acworth as part of the first course, or as a 'remove' brought to the table immediately after the soup. The Fish Sauce might have been poured over a baked carp or served beside it. All fish dishes would have been considered suitable for fasting days, pickled herrings in particular being traditional Lenten fare.

Chickens provided the most readily available and reliable meat. There were hen coops all over London, though the poulterers' shops of Westminster were concentrated mainly in the parish of St George's. The prudent housewife would still beware of fowls that were less than fresh and would look for smooth legs and short spurs as the sign of a young bird. The same applied to turkeys, which were driven along the roads to London from East Anglia in large flocks, taking up to three months on the journey. Setting off in August at the end of the harvest, they arrived in London in good time to be fattened up for Christmas. Geese too were in plentiful supply, but Mrs Acworth had only one recipe for this delicious bird, 'To Dry a Goose'. As it requires the bird to be rubbed with salt petre and powdered cochineal (dried Mexican insects used in making scarlet dye) and hung in a chimney to dry, it is not among her more compelling recipes and we have not included it. The remark in this recipe to dress the goose 'as you would doo to roast' suggests that she also served it in a more appetizing form. The object of drying, of course, was to be able to keep the goose in store for several months. On the day, she probably boiled the bird and served it with turnips, cabbage or other vegetables.

Poultry lends itself to the simplest and the most elaborate of cookery. Mrs Acworth no doubt roasted it on the spit as often as not, and put elderly birds into a pot with water and plenty of herbs to stew long and slowly. Of the recipes she gives, that for turkey pie, which we have renamed Grand Roast Turkey, is notable. The device of stuffing bigger birds with smaller birds was an ancient one. In the middle ages it was done with swans for very grand occasions. Mrs Acworth's turkey might have created a similar sensation at her own more modest table. The Stewed Chicken with Wine Sauce shows the common use of piquant flavours with boiling fowl, while the Pot-roasted Chicken or Guinea Fowl recipe uses Mrs Acworth's beloved mace and cloves in combination with herbs and wine to produce a different sort of spicy dish. (Guinea fowl, or Guinea hen as it is known in America, was introduced to Britain by the Romans but died out, not to return until the sixteenth century, when the Portuguese reintroduced it to Europe from Africa.) The fricassee dishes were blander, using large quantities of the cream which Mrs Acworth probably procured from the dairymen of St James's Park.

SAUSE FOR A COD'S HEAD Take a pint of White wine and a Lemmon sliced, half a pint of shrimps, a pint of Oysters with the Liquor of them, some large Mace and Nutmeg, 6 Anchoves, a little Horse Redish. Stew these together and Thicken them with 2 pounds of butter and 6 Yolks of Eggs. Boyle the cod in salt and water, lemmon Peal & sweete Hearbys. Garnesh the Dish with Shrimps, Oysters, Barburyes.

COD IN SHRIMP SAUCE

IN this recipe the strong spices and lavish use of wine which Mrs Acworth habitually used with fish work well. The egg yolks and butter soften and blend the flavours; and the textures of the shrimps, cod and thick, creamy sauce complement each other beautifully. It is one of our favourite fish recipes, equally good served in small quantities as a first course, or more generously as a main course. We have halved Mrs Acworth's quantities and suggest omitting the oysters, which would have been among the cheapest ingredients in her day. We also reduce the proportion of butter and we use cod fillet rather than cod's head, which would not have caused the sensation of surprise among Mrs Acworth's guests that might be expected among our own. (Cods' heads were commonly found on the eighteenth-century table. The delicate flesh of the cheeks was prized.) Since barberries, the bright red berries of the berberis shrub, are not easy to find, cranberries or red currants can be strewn across the dish to add the touch of colour that Mrs Acworth intended. This version makes an ample starter for six to eight people.

$\frac{1}{2}$ lemon
1$\frac{1}{2}$ lbs (675 g) cod fillet
1 tablespoon sea salt
2 bay leaves, 2 sprigs of thyme and some parsley, tied in
2 bunches
8 fl oz (225 ml, 1 cup) dry white wine
6 anchovy fillets
$\frac{1}{2}$ nutmeg
$\frac{1}{2}$ teaspoon ground mace
3 egg yolks
1 teaspoon flour
2 oz (60 g, $\frac{1}{4}$ cup) butter
$\frac{1}{2}$ lb (225 g) shrimps or prawns (unshelled weight)
one oyster for each person (optional)
1 tablespoon cranberries or red currants to garnish (optional)

Peel the lemon thinly and put pieces of the peel on top of the cod fillet in a shallow ovenproof dish. Sprinkle salt on the cod and arrange the bunches of herbs on top. Pour one or two spoonfuls of water over the fish, cover with foil and put it to bake in a fairly slow oven (gas mark 2, 300°F, 150°C) for 30 minutes. Put the wine in a saucepan with the anchovy fillets, spices and the peeled lemon cut into thin slices. Bring these to the boil and allow them to bubble vigorously for 5 to 10 minutes. Meanwhile mix the egg yolks, butter and flour together in a bowl. Remove the wine from the heat and let it cool slightly. Strain it over the egg yolks, butter and flour, whisking vigorously, and return the whole mixture to the saucepan. Stir or gently whisk the sauce over a low heat until it is quite thick, being careful not to let it boil. Set it to one side, and when the cod is cooked pour off some of its juice into the sauce. If the sauce needs thickening again, return it to a low heat and stir for a few more minutes. Peel the shrimps or prawns, leaving one in its skin for each person for decoration, and stir the peeled ones into the sauce. Pour the whole sauce over the cod, garnish with the unpeeled shrimps, some cranberries or red currants and oysters if you are using them, and serve immediately.

STEW'D SOLES Take a pair of Large soles, skin and dry them, then make a strong gravy of Beef, adding to it half a pint of Madeira Wine some shalots, mushrooms and spice to your palate, in which the soles must Stew till tender, and then serve them up; garnish with Parsley and Lemon.

BAKED SOLES

THIS recipe will serve four. It produces a simple dish of some delicacy.

2 whole (Dover) soles
16 fl oz (450 ml, 1 US pint) beef stock
8 fl oz (225 ml, 1 US cup) Madeira or sweet sherry
2 oz (60 g, ¼ cup) butter
4 shallots
2 oz (60 g) mushrooms
salt and freshly ground white pepper
parsley and lemon to garnish

Butter an ovenproof dish and put the soles, seasoned with salt and pepper, gently into it. Slice the shallots and mushrooms and fry them in butter. Add the beef stock and Madeira or sherry to this and pour it into the dish with the soles, making sure to have enough to cover them. Bake the soles until tender: about 15 minutes at gas mark 4 (350°F, 180°C). Serve them garnished with parsley and lemon. The sauce may be served separately with rice.

To STEW FRENCH CARP OR EELS Take half clarit and half water, 2 or 3 Anchovies, one Onion stuck with Cloves, a blade of Mace, whole pepper, a Little Lemon peal, a bunch of Sweet Yearbs. Lett the Liquor just cover it. Lett it stew gently and when half done turn them and Lett it stew till they are ready. The less Liquor you can stew them in the better. Take as Much Liquor as you think proper and Butter according to the Quantity of your fish with the yolk of an Egg or two. Melt your butter in the Liquor and When done beat up your egg and stir it well in, then Lett it boyle and pour it on the fish. If large you should blood it under the fins then putt in into the stewing.

CARP OR EELS IN WINE SAUCE

CARP and eels were much in favour in the eighteenth century. The fishponds of country houses supplied carp to families of the gentry and middle classes at a time when sea fish were still only available fresh for those who lived within a few hours' distance of the sea. Eels were a cheap and nutritious food eaten by people of all classes. They were shipped to London from the Fens or the Netherlands and were popular in pies, soups, pickles and stews. This recipe applies to carp as well as eels, but the carp needs cooking for about an hour, as opposed to the 20 minutes or so needed for the eels. It will serve eight or more. (There is considerably more waste on a carp than on eels.)

2 lb eels or 1 carp weighing 5 or 6 lbs (about 2.5 kg)
8 fl oz (225 ml, 1 cup) claret
8 fl oz (225 ml, 1 cup) water
2 or 3 anchovies
1 small onion
6 cloves
$\frac{1}{4}$ teaspoon ground mace
$\frac{1}{4}$ teaspoon salt
12 peppercorns
grated rind of $\frac{1}{2}$ lemon
a bunch of herbs including parsley, thyme and bay leaf
2 oz (60 g, $\frac{1}{4}$ cup) butter
1 egg yolk
parsley and lemon to garnish

Clean and skin the eels, cut them into pieces and place them in an ovenproof pan into which you have poured the claret and water. If you are using carp, soak it for 2 or more hours in cold water with a tablespoon of vinegar to remove the slightly muddy taste, then put it whole in the pan with the claret and water. Add the anchovies, an onion stuck with cloves, mace, salt, peppercorns, lemon rind and bunch of herbs. The liquid should just cover the fish. Bake it at gas mark 4 (350°F, 180°C) for about 20 minutes for eels, 1 hour for carp. Remove the fish and strain about half the liquid into a saucepan. Add the butter to it and stir in the egg yolk. Continue stirring over a low heat until the sauce thickens slightly. The sauce may be poured over the fish or served separately. Garnish with lemon and parsley.

FISH SAUCE Take two Anchovies, dissolve them in half a pint of grevey then strain it. Ad one spoonfull or 2 of port wine, a little Nutmeg & ginger grated & thicken it with butter. Squese in some Lemmon to your tast.

FISH SAUCE

A VERY good sauce for serving in small quantities with grilled or fried fish, e.g. mackerel, mullet or firm-fleshed white fish such as cod or halibut.

2 salted anchovies
8 fl oz (225 ml, 1 cup) fish stock
1 tablespoon port (optional)
a little grated nutmeg, to taste
1 tablespoon grated fresh ginger
1 tablespoon butter, worked to a paste with the same quantity
of flour
1 tablespoon (or less) lemon juice

Boil the fish stock with the anchovies in it. They really do dissolve, and it is unnecessary to strain the stock. Stir in the port, nutmeg and grated ginger, then the butter and flour paste. Let the sauce thicken slowly while you stir it, then add the lemon juice a little at a time, tasting as you do so. The end result should be a fairly thin sauce in which the flavour of fresh ginger is just more discernible than any other. Offered to each guest to spoon over the fish, it takes the place of tartare sauce or a similar relish.

To BUTTER CRABS OR LOBSTERS Your Crabs or Lobsters being boyld and Cold, take all the meat out of the shell and of the claws & mince it small & putt it alltogether, & ad to it 2 or 3 spoonfulls Claret, a very little Vinigar, a little greated Nutmeg and salt. Make it hott then putt in butter melted with a anchovy & greavy & thicken it up with the yolk of an Ege & make it Hott. Then putt it alltogether in the largest shell & stick into it some peaces of thin tosted Bread & so send it up to the Table. You must not lett it boyle affter the butter & ege are putt into it.

BUTTERED CRABS

THIS was one of the recipes given to Mrs Acworth by her friend Betty Edmonds, who, it seems, took it from Eliza Smith's *The Compleat Housewife*. Both this and the lobster version given below make a distinguished start to a dinner party. Both recipes provide generous portions for a first course for six people, and both can be served equally well hot or cold.

1 lb (450 g) fresh or frozen crabmeat
3 tablespoons red wine
1 tablespoon vinegar
$\frac{1}{2}$ nutmeg
$\frac{1}{2}$ teaspoon salt
1 teaspoon anchovy essence, or 2 anchovy fillets
1 egg yolk
4 oz (115 g, $\frac{1}{2}$ cup) butter
toast, lemon and parsley to garnish

Beat all the ingredients together well, or blend them in a food processor. Heat them gently in a saucepan, stirring occasionally. Pile the mixture into crab or scallop shells or some other suitable small dishes, and serve with triangles of toast, garnished with thin slices of lemon and a sprig of parsley.

BUTTERED LOBSTERS

USE 2 small cooked lobsters weighing about 1 lb (450 g) each, or one much larger one weighing twice as much, instead of the crabmeat. Having extracted the flesh from the lobsters, proceed exactly as for buttered crabs, but if you are not using a food processor, mince the lobster meat first.

Buttered Crab

To SEASON A TURKEY PYE Bone it and plump it and stick the breast with cloves. Season it with pepper salt and mace, then Lard & season A duck & putt in the turkey Belly. Lay it in the pye & fill up the corners of the Pye with forse Meat Balls putt in good store of Butter, Close it & Bake it.

GRAND ROAST TURKEY

THIS noble composition may have been thought too fragile to roast on a spit, where it might not have kept its shape in its boneless state. It therefore went into the bread oven in a pie. We have not found this recipe anywhere else, though Charles Carter's *The Complete Practical Cook* has a similar one without forcemeat (stuffing) balls. In our version we recommend roasting it with the forcemeat stuffed into the middle of the duck, for no modern domestic pie dish could accommodate it. The quantities given here would serve about twenty people. The recipe is equally good eaten cold and involves almost no waste.

> 1 turkey weighing about 12 lbs or 5.5 kg
> 1 duck weighing about 5 lbs or 2.25 kg
> forcemeat made with 12 oz (335 g) minced (ground) veal
> (see p. 63)
> 1 teaspoon ground mace
> 10 cloves
> salt and pepper
> watercress and slices of French bread or Manchet (see p. 94)
> to garnish

Ask your butcher to bone a turkey and a duck, leaving only the bones of the turkey wings in place. If you supply the forcemeat, he will probably put together the whole stuffed turkey for you. (The duck will not need larding unless it is a wild one.) Shape any remaining forcemeat into small balls, to be fried for 10 minutes and served round the turkey as part of the garnish. Stick about 10 cloves into the turkey breast, season with salt, pepper and mace and cover the whole bird with lightly buttered foil. Cook the stuffed turkey at gas mark 3 (325°F, 170°C) for 25 minutes per pound of its total weight, removing the foil about half an hour before it is finished. It is important to cook the bird at an even, moderate temperature, and if possible use a meat thermometer to make sure it is cooked through. Serve garnished with slices of French bread or Manchet lightly fried in butter, a few sprigs of watercress, and Forcemeat balls.

TO BAKE ALL SORTS OF SMALL FOWLS Take your fowles and lard them. Stick some with Bacon and some with lemon peel and some cloves and with pepper, salt, Mace and Nutmeg beaten. Season your fowles and in every fowles belly put a Clove of Garlick wrapped in a Sage Leafe and a bay Leafe. In butter put into them and so lay the fowle close in an earthen pott and put so much butter in as will bake them Moist. Put in a little ffrench wine to bake with them. When you have taken them out of the oven pour ffrom them all the butter and Gravy that will run from them then separate the butter from the liquor and put it into the pott againe.

POT-ROASTED CHICKEN OR GUINEA FOWL

THIS recipe can be used for any sort of 'small fowl' including game birds. If you use more than one bird, you can follow Mrs Acworth's instructions to the letter, putting bacon under the skin of one and lemon rind under the skin of another. The recipe makes enough juice to serve as a gravy for the accompanying rice, noodles or potatoes. Although Mrs Acworth seems to have served the fowl in its pot, it graces the dinner table just as well and is easier to serve placed on a carving dish surrounded with Forcemeat balls (see p. 63) and little sippets (triangles) of bread fried in butter or oil.

1 medium-sized chicken or guinea fowl (guinea hen)
1 slice of bacon
rind of $\frac{1}{2}$ lemon
$\frac{1}{4}$ teaspoon ground cloves plus 2 whole ones
about $\frac{1}{2}$ teaspoon each of ground black pepper, salt, mace and nutmeg
1 bay leaf
1 sage leaf, or a pinch of ground dried sage
1 clove of garlic
2 oz (60 g, $\frac{1}{4}$ cup) butter
1 wine glass full of dry red or white wine

Cut the bacon and lemon rind into small pieces and stick them under the skin of the bird. Mix together the ground cloves, pepper, salt and nutmeg, and distribute some of this mixture under the skin, reserving the rest to rub on top. Attach the bay leaf and sage leaf to the clove of garlic with a couple of cloves and place inside the bird. Rub the rest of the seasoning into the skin. Melt the butter in a casserole, brown the bird in it, then pour the wine over. Let this come rapidly to the boil. Cover the casserole and put it in a moderate oven (gas mark 2, 300°F, 150°C) to cook for about $1\frac{1}{2}$ hours.

TO MAKE A WHITE FRIGACY Take your Chickin & cutt it into small peaces & wash the Blood clean from it. Sett it over the fier with water just to cover it. Putt pepper salt & a bunch of time & a whole Oinion. When it is stewed tender have redy the yolks of three Egs beaten with some of the Liquor, putt in parsley chop'd a little white wine & a spoonfull of Vinigar, greated nutmeg, a peace of fresh butter and a anchove chop'd. Mix all these together over the fier till you think it is thick anuff. You must putt in your meat & let it boyle Halfe an Ower, then putt into it Half a pint of Cream & stir it well together over the fire & searve it up.

WHITE FRICASSEE

FRICASSEE appeared in English cookery during the sixteenth century, having originated in France. According to Anne Wilson's *Food and Drink in Britain*, it was originally a dish of various meats cooked together, but had come by the eighteenth century to be often a simple dish of chicken or rabbit with a creamy sauce. This recipe is simple to make, but the combination of vinegar, anchovies, nutmeg and white wine, together with the herbs, make it distinctive. The strong flavours of the vinegar and anchovies are masked by the cream added at the end, so that the final result is soft but subtle.

1 large chicken, cut into pieces
pepper and salt to taste
1 large onion
a large bunch of fresh thyme, or 1 tablespoon dried thyme
3 egg yolks
about 1 cup of chopped parsley
4 fl oz (115 g, ½ cup) dry white wine
1 tablespoon white wine vinegar
about ½ nutmeg
1 oz (30 g, 1 tablespoon) butter
4 small anchovy fillets, chopped very small
8 fl oz (225 ml, 1 cup) single (light) cream
parsley to garnish

Cover the chicken joints with water in a saucepan, add salt and pepper and the onion and thyme, bring to the boil and then allow to simmer gently for about 45 minutes, until the chicken is tender but still quite firm. Take about 16 fl oz (450 ml, 2 cups or 1 US pint) of the liquid in which the chicken cooked, and stir in the egg yolks, using a wire whisk. Add all the other ingredients except the cream, place them in a saucepan over a moderate heat and stir gently until the mixture thickens (about 5 to 10 minutes). Do not allow it to boil because this would make it curdle.

Place the chicken joints in an ovenproof dish and cover them with the thickened mixture and then with a lid or piece of foil. Bake at gas mark 4 (350°F, 180°C) for 20 minutes. Remove the dish from the oven and stir in the cream. Return it to the oven for 10 more minutes to heat the cream. Garnish with chopped parsley.

A FRICACY OF CHICKENS OR RABETTS Cutt your Chickens into quarters and throw em into cold water. Let 'em lye in it ¹/₂ an Hour, then put a quarter of a pound of butter into a fflat bottomed saucepan and let it boyle. So put your Chickins into ye boyling Butter and let 'em boyle till they are ¹/₂ enough. Then put to 'em ¹/₂ a pint of White Broath, yt is if you have Mutton Veale or Lamb boyling at that time, if not soo much Warme water will doo, and a little Shred parsley, an Onion. So let it boyle till it is enough, then to every Chickin you Must put ye yolke of an Egg to thicken it up, then add ye juice of Lemon and 2 or 3 spoonfulls of Creame. So shake it very well together.

FRICASSEE OF CHICKEN OR RABBIT

LIKE the White Fricassee, this one is very straightforward. Rice and green peas or a salad make a good accompaniment.

1 large chicken or rabbit, cut into pieces
4 oz (115 g, ½ cup) butter
salt and pepper to taste
4 fl oz (115 ml, ½ cup) double (heavy) cream
1 egg yolk
2 tablespoons lemon juice

Melt the butter over a moderate heat until it foams but without letting it turn brown. Throw in the joints of chicken or rabbit, and cook them at the same heat for about 30 minutes. Add salt and pepper and the cream mixed with the lightly beaten egg yolk. Stir well, reduce the heat and cook for another 30 minutes with a lid over the pan. When the meat is tender, stir in the lemon juice, adjust the seasoning to taste, shake the pan well, and serve.

SAUSE FOR A HEN Take the Yolks of 3 or 4 eggs, some butter and four spoonfulls of Claret wine, some grave & the juce of a lemmon.

STEWED CHICKEN WITH WINE SAUCE

THE hen for which this sauce was intended would have been a boiling fowl, a reasonably old chicken and perhaps culled from the coop because it was past its best at laying eggs. Although its meat needed long cooking to make it tender, it would have been prized for its flavour. Nowadays such birds rarely find their way into the shops, but it still is worth cooking younger chickens in a simple stock of water, herbs, carrot and onion, especially if they are to be served with a sauce like this.

1 chicken
water to cover
1 onion
1 carrot
a bunch of herbs including bay leaf, thyme, rosemary and parsley
salt and pepper to taste
FOR THE SAUCE:
3 egg yolks
1 oz (30 g, 1 tablespoon) butter
4 tablespoons red wine
4 fl oz (115 ml, ½ cup) chicken stock
2 tablespoons lemon juice

Cover the chicken with water, add the herbs and the carrot and onion, chopped into large pieces, season to taste with salt and pepper, bring to the boil and then simmer for 1 to 1½ hours, according to the size of the chicken. When the chicken is nearly cooked, prepare the sauce. Beat together the egg yolks and softened butter with a wire whisk. Add the lemon juice. Bring the chicken stock and wine to the boil and allow them to bubble rapidly for a few moments. Let the liquid cool down for 2 or 3 minutes, then pour it on to the egg yolks, beating well with the whisk. Return the mixture to the saucepan over a low heat and stir constantly until the sauce has thickened to a consistency like custard. Serve it either separately in a bowl, or spooned over the chicken. It is pink in colour and piquant in flavour.

To MAKE CHICKEN PYE Bruse the bones of some & joynt the rest. Season them with pepper, Cloves, Mace & Nutmegs, some sweet hearbs shreed small. Fill the pye with a dish of Butter and when it is Baked Disolve two anchoves in half a pint of White Wine, one Shallot. So putt in the pye Hott.

CHICKEN PIE

HERE is a delicious and straightforward recipe, which will serve six people. The flavour is spicy but not so strong as to overwhelm the delicacy of the chicken. Cooked in a raised pie it looks superb, and the contents emerge from within their golden-brown crust tender and aromatic.

raised pie crust made with 12 oz (340 g, 2¼ cups) flour (see p. 75)
6 boned chicken breasts, or 12 smaller chicken pieces
2 oz (60 g, ¼ cup) butter
½ teaspoon each of ground pepper, cloves, mace and nutmeg
1 tablespoon each chopped fresh or 1 teaspoon each of dried
marjoram, parsley and rosemary
1 egg yolk mixed with 1 tablespoon milk, to glaze the pastry
8 fl oz (225 ml, 1 cup) white wine
1 shallot
4 anchovy fillets

Line a raised pie mould with the pastry (see p. 75), or make a pie shell by moulding the pastry round the outside of a cake tin. (We used an oval mould 5½ × 9 inch, 14 × 23 cm.) Melt a little of the butter in a frying pan and brown the pieces of chicken lightly in it. Lift them out and season them with the pepper, cloves, mace and nutmeg mixed together. Put them into the pie mould and sprinkle the chopped herbs over them. Dot the contents of the pie with small pieces of butter and place the pastry lid over the top, taking care not to seal it down so firmly that you will not be able to lift it off when it has cooked. Brush the top with a mixture of beaten egg yolk and milk and put it in the oven to cook at gas mark 5 (375°F, 190°C) for 30 minutes. Meanwhile, chop the shallot and anchovy fillets finely and put them in a saucepan with the wine. Bring to the boil and let them bubble fast for about 2 minutes. Keep the mixture warm until you are ready to add it to the pie. After the pie has cooked for 30 minutes remove it from the oven. If you are using a metal pie mould, remove the sides carefully so that the pastry inside will have a chance to brown, and brush with the remaining mixture of egg yolk and milk. Gently lift off the pastry lid and pour in the hot wine with the shallot and anchovy dissolved in it. Replace the lid and put the pie back in the oven, standing in a roasting dish in case it leaks, at gas mark 3 (325°F, 170°C) for about 20 minutes.

CHAPTER THREE

MEAT AND

GAME

Scotch Collops
White Veal Escalopes
Veal or Pork Olives
Ragout of Veal
Forcemeat
Potted Beef
Spiced Beef in Red Wine
Collared Venison
Lamb Haricot
Ham Pie
Pigeons in Scallop Shells
Hare with Cream Sauce
Pastry for Raised Pies

Pigeon in Scallop Shell; Ham Pie; Scotch Collops, Rachel Manaton

THE aroma of roasting meat must have been one of the characteristic smells in the homes of well-to-do people in eighteenth-century London. It wafted along passages and upstairs from the great open fires of the kitchens, where haunches of venison and sides of beef, lamb and pork roasted on spits. The Acworths' house in Smith Street was no exception. Some of Mrs Acworth's recipes show that she used a spit with a dripping pan beneath, from which the juices would have been spooned over the meat as it roasted. But this all-important element in her cooking did not require recipes. She wasted no space on instructions for the most basic of skills. Her numerous meat recipes almost all call for cooking in an oven or a pot, or for curing in brine or smoking over a wood fire. They are usually for composite dishes using more than one sort of meat and calling for sauces and ragouts which blend together several different herbs and seasonings.

Veal takes up a large proportion of the meat recipes in Mrs Acworth's book. She did roast it, at least as a preliminary to turning it into a ragout, but more often she cooked it in 'collops' or fricandos, or minced it up and made it into forcemeat (stuffing). Veal had the merit of being a soft, tender meat, bland in itself, and therefore the perfect foil for culinary art. When her guests had helped themselves to the great roast centrepiece of the first course, Mrs Acworth might have invited them to turn their attention to the more delicate side dishes, usually including one at least of veal with its appetizing hint of mace, wine and herbs, elegantly arranged on a platter and surrounded by mushrooms and slices of orange or lemon. She had several good recipes for Scotch Collops, a classic of eighteenth-century cookery. 'Collop' was an old English name for a slice of meat, and these versions may have been called Scotch because they were scotched, or 'hacked' with the side of a knife to flatten them. Forcemeat balls were the constant companion of Scotch Collops, as well as turning up in soups and pies and alongside fowl and other meats. Knuckle of veal, meanwhile, formed the basis of the soups and broths with which the meal began, and which also went into the making of sauces for the other meat dishes.

Of the other staple meats in the modern diet there is relatively little. Mutton, which was taken from much older animals than modern lamb, and tasted much stronger, appears occasionally as an alternative to veal but otherwise only in the rather good 'herricoe' and in a curious recipe which we have not included, 'to make Dutch beef'. Beef itself appears in various forms. It is cured and potted to make a simple pâté, or stuck with herbs and spices and stewed in claret. It too is used in soup, and the gravy which Mrs Acworth uses liberally in her sauces probably came from roasting beef. In the hierarchy of meats, beef must have come above mutton, for while mutton is used in 'Dutch beef', beef is used to make

'Red deer' (neither included here). Pork is to be found in the shape of ham, brawn (head cheese) and bacon and in a recipe to 'make pork like Westphalia ham', but nowhere among the more elegant side dishes. In modern cookery it substitutes well for veal, and it can certainly be used in Mrs Acworth's Scotch Collop recipes, but we have found no sign that she did so herself.

The two main sorts of game used by Mrs Acworth were venison and hare. Venison was an expensive luxury by her time, for the few remaining wild herds were to be found almost exclusively in the wilds of Exmoor and in certain parts of Scotland. Furthermore, a succession of game laws had attached increasingly ferocious penalties to poaching during the lifetimes of herself and her parents. She may have had access to venison from private game parks, however, for in one or two of her recipes she varies the instructions according to whether the deer had been hunted or not. (She says the meat of the hunted deer did not need beating to make it tender.) Hare was more easily obtained, although it too fell within the scope of the more recent game laws. It was commonly cooked in its own juices in a jug, inside a cauldron or large pot in which puddings and other dishes might be cooking. Mrs Acworth had recipes for doing other interesting things with hare, including the Hare with Cream Sauce which we give here. This recipe, like the one for collared venison, is well worth reviving, provided always that one has the time and patience for the long, slow cooking that game generally needs. The same applies to the pigeon recipes, although since pigeons are small they do not need cooking for as long as hare or venison. We have included them as game rather than fowl because Mrs Acworth's pigeons would almost certainly have been wood pigeon, shot in the wild, and her recipes could have been used equally well for partridges or other small game birds.

No collection of meat recipes from the eighteenth century is complete without some pies. Pies are the stuff of legend and nursery rhyme. They are also a good way of cooking meat in the oven without allowing it to become dry; and once cooked, they are an admirable device for keeping their contents fresh. Before the days of oven-roasting and refrigerators, they were a practical necessity. Fine, upstanding pies of giant size would have been available almost constantly in prosperous larders. They were there to grace the dinner table at first serving and then to be sliced cold for a snack or a supper, probably for the meals of the domestic staff as much as for the owners of the house and their family. The strong pastry made with suet (kidney fat) which encased them would be moulded around the shape of a cake hoop, or coaxed into a fluted mould, and decorated with whatever shapes the cook's imagination might call forth. From several tempting recipes in Mrs Acworth's manuscript we have included the Ham Pie, her version of a classic dish.

SCOTCH COLLOPS, COUSIN R. MANATON Take the quantity you want of Veal, cutt it in slices as Thin as possible. Flower them very well and fry them in a Little Butter, and Browne of a Light colour. Whilst frying, season them with pepper & salt. When done pour the grease from them & add as much good gravey as will make a sufficient sauce & keep tossing them till they are of a proper thickness. Then putt in an Onion, Time, Mushrooms, Truffels & Morells and Artichoke Bottoms cutt in Dice & boiled tender, Sweetbreads, coxcombs & force Meat Balls and some thin slices of Baken. Before it is served. up, squeese in the juce of a small Lemmon & a little White wine if you like it. Garnish the dish with Bacon & slised. Lemmon or Barberys if you have them.

SCOTCH COLLOPS

Mrs Acworth's cousin, Rachel Manaton, supplied her with some relatively elaborate recipes. This one, though not complicated to prepare, calls for numerous different ingredients. It is worth the trouble, for the combination of flavours and textures works well and, piled on a good-sized meat plate and decorated with Forcemeat balls and slices of lemon, it presents a most impressive appearance. We have omitted the cocks' combs, truffles and morels only because they are difficult to obtain. Cranberries or red currants can be used in place of barberries (see p. 42).

6 veal escalopes (scallops), each weighing not more than 3 oz (85 g)
and beaten flat
about 3 tablespoons flour
2 oz (60 g, $\frac{1}{4}$ cup) butter
8 fl oz (225 g, 1 cup) chicken stock
1 medium onion
4 oz (225 g) sweetbreads, soaked in cold water for 2 hours
3 thin slices of bacon
1 tablespoon dried or 2 tablespoons chopped fresh thyme
4 oz (115 g) field mushrooms
6 artichoke hearts or bottoms
forcemeat made with 8 oz (225 g) pie veal (diced shoulder or
breast of veal) (see p. 63)
2 small lemons
4 fl oz (115 ml, $\frac{1}{2}$ cup) dry white wine
2 tablespoons cranberries or red currants (optional)

Cut each escalope into 3 or 4 pieces and cover them well in flour. Season them lightly with salt and pepper and fry them for about 5 minutes on each side in melted butter, until they are golden brown. Set them to one side on a dish, and pour the chicken stock into the pan in which they cooked. Bring this to the boil and add the finely chopped onion. Cook this until the onion is soft (about 5 minutes), stirring well as the sauce thickens. Meanwhile prepare the sweetbreads, which you have soaked in cold water for 2 hours, by blanching them in boiling water for 2 minutes, removing the membranes and cutting them into dice. Fry the bacon slices in another pan until they are crisp, and cut them into small bits. Add to the sauce the chopped sweetbreads, small pieces of bacon, thyme, mushrooms and diced artichokes and stir in the lemon juice and wine. Bring the sauce with all its ingredients to the boil and let it bubble for about 2 minutes. Then pour it over the slices of cooked veal. Garnish with Forcemeat balls which have been cooked separately (see p. 63) and thin slices of lemon, plus cranberries or red currants if you wish.

*TO MAKE WHITE SCOTCH COLLOPS Take a Leg of veal &
cutt your Collops of thin. Hack ym with the back of a knife then Season ym &
fry ym with beaten butter butt nott brown. Then have reddy some Lemmon
peal, white wine, a blade of Mace. Thicken it up with butter rold in flower. Dish
it up with Mushrooms, Lemmon cutt in slices & force Meat balls.*

WHITE VEAL ESCALOPES

THIS, the less elaborate of the two recipes for Scotch Collops which we
have selected from several in Mrs Acworth's book, is quick, easy
and delicious. The sauce clearly was meant to look creamy white,
surrounded by the contrasting colours of the mushrooms, Forcemeat
balls and lemon slices.

6 escalopes (scallops) of veal or pork, each weighing about
3 oz (85 g)
salt and pepper
about 2 oz (60 g, ¼ cup) butter
grated zest of 1 small or ½ a large lemon
2 teaspoons ground mace
1 wine glass full of dry white wine, or half a glass of dry sherry
about 1 tablespoon white flour
6 slices of lemon
about 2 oz (60 g) mushrooms
Forcemeat balls (see p. 63) to garnish

Season the escalopes lightly with salt and pepper (white pepper if you are
going to be perfectionist). Heat the butter in a frying pan until it froths
but is not brown, and fry the escalopes until each one is cooked. Place
them in the oven in the dish in which you mean to serve them, to keep
warm while you make the sauce. Sprinkle the flour over the juices in the
pan, adding a little more butter if necessary, stir in the lemon zest, mace
and finally the wine, and cook until it forms a smooth sauce. Pour the
sauce over the escalopes and garnish the dish with slices of lemon, fried
mushrooms and Forcemeat balls.

VEAL OLIVES Take a Leg of veal & Cutt thin Large Slices & beat them with a rolling pin. Then take thin slices of bacon & lay on the Veal, then season it with sweet yerbs, a little greated bread, some Nutmeg, a little Lemmon peal cut fine, salt & pepper. Strew it upon your meet, role it up & tye it, then dip them in yolk of eggs with grated bread sifted over them. Note a quarter of an hour bakes them. Putt them in a cleen dish & poor over them the same sauce as for Scoth Collops & ad force meat Balls. N.B. Your oven must be heated in the same manner as for Tarts.

VEAL OR PORK OLIVES

THIS delicious variation on the recipes for Scotch Collops is reminiscent of modern Italian cooking. The combination of veal, bacon and breadcrumbs mixed with herbs works well and looks most attractive as you slice into it on your plate. Served with all the trimmings of Forcemeat balls and one of the sauces given in the recipes for Scotch Collops, the following quantities make a hearty meal for six people.

6 escalopes (scallops) of veal or pork, each weighing about
3 oz (85 g)
12 slices of bacon
about ½ nutmeg
about 4 oz (115 g, 2 cups) fresh breadcrumbs
grated zest of ½ a large lemon
about ½ cup each fresh thyme and parsley
salt and pepper
1 whole egg plus 2 egg yolks
a little olive oil or butter
Forcemeat balls (see p. 63), or mushrooms and lemon slices
to garnish

Beat the escalopes out on a board until they are quite thin. Lay 2 bacon slices over each one and grate nutmeg over each. Mix the freshly grated breadcrumbs with the lemon zest, herbs and seasonings, and stir in a lightly beaten egg to bind the mixture. Pile a portion of the mixture on each escalope, roll them up and tie them tightly with string. Roll each 'olive' in the lightly beaten yolks of two eggs and then in breadcrumbs. Fry them lightly in very hot oil or butter, place in a shallow ovenproof dish dotted with butter, and bake for 20 to 30 minutes at gas mark 4 (350°F, 180°C). Serve with Forcemeat balls and one of the sauces described in the recipes for Scotch Collops, or garnished simply with fried mushrooms and slices of lemon.

To RAGOUT A BREAST OF VEAL Take a Breast of veal & Roast it very Brown. Then take a ladle of good gravey and another of Strong Broth, cut yr. veal in half & put it in a stewpan & stove it down till tis very tender. Get some sweetbreads, morrells, muchrooms, artychoke bottoms & force meat Balls. Squeze in a little lemmon, thicken it with a bit of butter Roll'd in flour. This is an exceeding Good Receipt.

RAGOUT OF VEAL

THIS is indeed an exceeding good receipt. Served with the artichoke hearts, mushrooms and Forcemeat balls surrounding the veal and a little of the sauce spooned over it, it looks very fine, tastes delicious and serves six.

1 joint of veal, weighing about 2½ lbs (1.15 kg) (if breast of veal is
unobtainable, shoulder does very well)
8 oz (225 g) sweetbreads, soaked in cold water with a dash of
lemon juice for 2 hours
4 oz (115 g) mushrooms
1 large tin of artichoke hearts (about 1 lb, 450 g)
1 cup each of strong beef stock (made from a cube if necessary)
and Strong Broth (see p. 32)
½ lemon
1 teaspoon butter or margarine
1 tablespoon flour
at least 1 Forcemeat ball per person, to garnish (see p. 63)

Roast the veal for 1 hour at gas mark 4 (350°F, 180°C), turning it once or twice to make sure it is brown all over. When you remove it from the oven and cut it in half, it should be barely pink in the middle. While the veal is roasting, prepare the sweetbreads by blanching them for 2 minutes in boiling water, then removing the membranes and cutting them into small dice. Wash the mushrooms and rinse the artichokes well. When the veal is ready, cut it in half and place the two pieces in a large casserole or ovenproof saucepan. Put the sweetbreads, mushrooms and artichoke hearts into the casserole with the veal and cover it all with the beef stock and Strong Broth mixed together. (Beef stock alone will do if you do not happen to have Strong Broth already made, but the broth lends distinction to the end result.) Stir in the juice of half a lemon. Cover the casserole and put it in the oven to cook for another 30 minutes at gas mark 4 (350°F, 180°C). The Forcemeat balls can roast in the top part of the oven at the same time. When the meat is very tender, remove it from the casserole and place it on a meat dish, putting it back in the oven at a very low temperature to keep warm. Mash together the butter or margarine and flour, and stir them into the sauce over a moderate heat. Bring it slowly to the boil, stirring well, and allow it to thicken for a minute or two. Spoon some of the sauce over the veal and arrange the other ingredients, including the Forcemeat balls, round it.

THE FORCED MEAT Beef Suit is better than fatt of Loyle of Veal. A little veal, thin winter savory, parsley, lemmon peal, mace, cuian, Salt, a glass of Madera Wine, no Bread. Mix these together with an Egg and make it up in Balls. Putt them in your Dish with Yolk of Egg boyld hard & bake it. Some People fry the forced Meat & putt it into the Dish when it comes from the oven.

FORCEMEAT

M RS Acworth gives several recipes for forcemeat. This one, which seems the tastiest, was meant to go with 'English Turtle' which she made with boiled calf's head (see p. 37). The hard-boiled egg yolks which appear in the recipe presumably were intended as a garnish for the English Turtle, so we have left them out. We have served it in balls as a garnish to Pot-roasted Fowl and used it as the stuffing for Grand Roast Turkey (see pp. 49 and 48). Forcemeat balls are also good as a snack, and almost as appetizing cold as hot. The mixture freezes well, so it is worth while making plenty.

12 oz (340 g) pie veal (diced shoulder or breast of veal)
1 small onion
3 oz (85 g, about 1½ cups) fresh breadcrumbs
3 oz (85 g, 1 cup) shredded suet (kidney fat)
grated zest of ½ a lemon
1 tablespoon each of ground mace and dried winter savory
1 teaspoon each of sea salt and ground Cayenne pepper
chopped parsley to taste
pepper to taste
1 egg
2 fl oz (60 ml, ¼ cup) port or Madeira
2 tablespoons flour

Mince the veal and onion together, stir in the breadcrumbs, suet, lemon zest and seasonings. Stir in the egg and lastly the Madeira or port. Form the mixture into small balls, flour them lightly and bake in the oven for about 30 minutes with whatever meat you are roasting (e.g. at gas mark 4, 350°F, 180°C).

TO POT MEATE Take a Ache bone peice of beefe and cut out ye bone. Then stab it well with a knife, then take salt peeter and beate it small and Mingle it with other salt. Then salt it well for 6 days and put it into a pot with a little pump water. Then bake it well with your household bread and when it is baked well take it out of your pot into a Cleane Dish and bruise it all to peeces. Then put it into a pot agreeable to your Meate and press it downe Hard with your hand, and Melt a pound of fresh butter with your grated nutmeg and cover it with bay leaves.

POTTED BEEF

THIS is a simple and excellent recipe. It is even simpler if you take the short cut of using beef that has already been salted for you, though the process of salting your own beef is interesting and not complicated. The saltpetre helps to give it its distinctive bright red colour. The herbs, which we have added, give a pretty variegated effect as well as a good flavour.

a piece of beef brisket weighing approximately 4 lbs (1.8 kg)
½ oz (15 g, 1 tablespoon) powdered saltpetre (potassium nitrate)
1 lb (450 g) common kitchen salt, or fine sea salt
bay leaves, thyme and parsley to taste
1 nutmeg, grated
8 oz (225 g, 1 cup) butter

Rub the beef well all over with the mixture of salt and saltpetre; make incisions at intervals all over it and rub some more of the mixture into them. Leave the meat in a refrigerator for 6 days. Alternatively, buy a piece of salt beef. Cover the salted beef with water, adding several bay leaves if you wish, bring to the boil, skim and leave it to cook over a gentle heat for at least 2½ hours. When it is well cooked, remove it from the saucepan and chop or mince it very finely. Stir in chopped thyme and parsley and grated nutmeg, and spoon the mixture into a large terrine or loaf tin, pressing it down firmly with your knuckles as you do so. Place two or three bay leaves on top, melt the butter and pour it through a sieve over the beef. Well covered in the refrigerator, the potted beef will keep well for at least a week. Serve it as you would a pâté, with bread or toast, as a snack or first course.

Veal Olives; Potted Beef

To STEW A RUMP OF BEEFF Having boil'd it till it is little more than half enough, take it up and peele of the Skin. Take salt, Pepper, beaten mace, grat'd nutmeg, a handfull of Parsley; a little Thyme, Winter Savoury, Sweet marjoram, all chopt fine and mixt, and stuff them in great holes, in the fat and lean. The rest spread over it with the Yolks of two eggs. Save the gravy that runs out, put to it a Pint of Claret (or red wine will do as well) and put the [beef] in a deep Pan. Pour the Liquor in, cover it close and let it bake two hours. Then put it in the dish and pour the liquor over it and send it to Table.

SPICED BEEF IN RED WINE

THIS is an excellent and unusual recipe which serves six people. It is just as good eaten cold as hot.

1 joint of beef (rump, sirloin or brisket) weighing about
2½ lbs (1.15 kg)
½ teaspoon each of salt, pepper, ground mace and ground
nutmeg, dried thyme, winter savory and marjoram
a large bunch of parsley, finely chopped
1 egg yolk
16 fl oz (450 ml, 2 cups or 1 US pint) red wine

Put the beef in a deep saucepan as near as possible to its own size, cover it with water, bring it to the boil, reduce the heat and leave it to simmer for 1 hour. While it is cooking, mix together the herbs and spices, including the chopped parsley. Mash them into a paste with the egg yolk. Remove the beef from the saucepan after an hour and allow it to cool slightly so that it can be handled. Using a sharp, pointed knife, make deep slits at spaces all over the meat. Push portions of the mixed herbs, spices and egg yolk deep into the slits, trying to make sure that it reaches the centre of the joint and is reasonably evenly distributed. Replace the meat in the saucepan and pour the wine over it, adding a little of the water in which it is first cooked if necessary so that the meat is completely covered. Bring it slowly to the boil and let it simmer gently over a low heat or in a moderate oven (gas mark 2, 300°F, 150°C) for 2 hours. The beef should be beautifully tender and aromatic by that time. Carve it on a meat platter and serve the sauce in a jug, to be poured over rice, noodles or mashed potatoes. Green salad makes a good accompaniment.

TO COLLAR VENISON Take your venison and bone it, then cut it in peices above ye breath of your hand. If it be not hunted, beate it with ye back of your Cleaver to make it tender. Season it with Reed Deer seasoning, then put into your pott one laying of fatt and another of Leane. If you please you may put in a Lay of Lard or two. Press it close in your pott till you think it full enough. Put in good store of butter. Pott up your pott. Lett it stand in your oven till it be very Tender. When you take it out, open your pott and pour out your gravey, then whilst it is Hott Lay on a Light Weight and press it close. Then fill it up with Clarified butter and if it be not Hunted, Soake it in pump Water.

COLLARED VENISON

To collar means literally to tie up meat in a circle before cooking it. Mrs Acworth used the word more loosely, as here, where the venison is certainly not tied into shape. She had recipes for collaring beef and fish as well as venison. What they had in common with this recipe was an end result of closely packed, well-flavoured meat which could be served cold in slices. The reference to 'red deer' seasoning leads to another recipe, where thin slices of lean beef are treated in much the same way to make mock 'red deer', seasoned 'high' with salt, pepper and cloves. This is a good way of cooking venison.

1 lb (450 g) very thinly sliced venison steak
2 oz (60 g, ¼ cup) pork fat or lard
8 oz (225 g) unsmoked fatty bacon
4 oz (115 g, ½ cup) butter
1 tablespoon freshly ground black pepper or 2 tablespoons
crushed green peppercorns
1 teaspoon fine sea salt
½ teaspoon ground cloves
a little pastry or flour-and-water paste
2 oz (60 g, ¼ cup) clarified butter

Lightly grease a small round casserole dish with butter. Place the venison, pork fat or lard and bacon in the dish in alternating layers, sprinkling some of the seasoning over each layer. Dot each layer of venison with a little butter cut into small dice. Press the meat down firmly. Seal the lid on the dish with a strip of pastry or flour-and-water paste. Cook for 4 hours at gas mark 2 (300°F, 150°C). Remove the lid when the dish is still hot, pour off all the liquid fat and cover the surface of the meat with a saucer or piece of greaseproof (waxed) paper, with a weight on top. Leave the meat to cool, then put it in the refrigerator, still under its weight, for about 24 hours. When you remove the weight, pour clarified butter on top of the meat and replace the lid. Serve this dish as you would a pâté, and offer red currant jelly as a relish.

A HERRICOE OF MUTTON Take a neck of mutton cut in thin cutlets, beat them flat and season them with pepper and salt, put a peice of butter & fry yr. cuttlets brown on both sides. When done, take them out and drain all the fat from them, then in another stewpan put a quarter of a pd. of Butter & a spatter full of flour & stir it well till tis Brown. Then put gravey to it as much as will cover the cuttlets, then scim it clean from fat & let them stew until they are quite tender. Then strain them again & scim yr. liquor Clean from fat. You must have some carrots, turnips Sallery &c. boil'd tender & put to yr. cutlets being all warmed together & yr. sauce as thick as Cream. Serve up hot.

To MAKE THE GRAVEY Take two onions & put them in the Bottom of a stewpan & 2 or 3 pd. of beef upon them. Carrots, turnips sallery thyme & Parsley strew over yr. beeff. Put about a gill of watter then cover yr. stew pan & put it over a slow fire till tis Brown at the Bottom. When Brown pour in as much Boiling water as will cover yr. herricoe. Strain it & scim of the Greasse well. An onion stuck with cloves is a great addition to the flavour.

LAMB HARICOT

Haricot was used much as ragout came to be used later, meaning a kind of stew with a smooth, creamy sauce (rather than the mixed meat sauce usually added to pies which the word ragout still defined in Mrs Acworth's vocabulary). It apparently had nothing to do with haricot beans. This recipe, which is not as complicated as it looks, is clearly related to Irish stew and Lancashire hot-pot, but notably more refined: Westminster's answer to its country cousins. It produces a delicious and distinctively flavoured dish.

12 lamb cutlets
salt and pepper
a little oil or butter for frying
1 tablespoon flour
8 oz (225 g) stewing beef or minced (ground) beef
3 onions
4 cloves
1 large carrot
1 large turnip
2 or 3 sticks of celery
a bunch of parsley and thyme
a little water
extra carrots, celery and turnips to garnish

Season the cutlets on both sides. Heat a very little butter or oil in a frying pan and when it is very hot, sear the cutlets in it so that they are brown on both sides. Place them in an ovenproof dish and sprinkle the flour over them. Set them to one side until the gravy is ready. To make this, chop up two of the onions and sprinkle them over the base of a heavy pan. Add the beef, then the third onion stuck with cloves and all the other ingredients, having chopped all except the herbs quite small. Pour over it all barely enough water to cover the bottom of the pan, then put on the lid and leave it to cook over a moderate heat, stirring from time to time. After about 30 minutes, the meat and vegetables should be beginning to stick to the bottom of the pan, giving off a strong savoury aroma. Pour enough boiling water over to cover them barely, scrape the bottom of the pan and stir well, then allow all to boil rapidly for a few moments. Remove the saucepan from the heat and strain the liquid into a bowl. Leave it to stand for a few minutes, then skim off the fat. Pour the skimmed liquid over the cutlets and place immediately in a fairly hot oven (gas mark 5, 375°F, 190°C). Cook for about 30 minutes, until the cutlets are tender. Remove them on to a serving dish and pour the sauce into a pan to boil and reduce for a few minutes, until it is the consistency of thin cream. Pour it over the cutlets and serve garnished with lightly boiled or steamed carrots, turnips and celery.

TO MAKE A HAM PYE Soak a ham one night, boyl it till it is very tender and then cutt of all the Rust and chop of every bone that looks awkward. Then put it into the pye seasond, with sweet Bassel and bay leaves and pepper. Dry them and rub them together till they are as fine as if Beating. When it comes from the Oven you must scum of the fat. Have your Ragout redy to put to it.

THE RAGOUT FOR THE HAM PYE This is a very good receipt of itself. Take some very strong broth seasond high with onion stuck with cloves, and a Bunch of sweet yearbs in a little of the liquor which the Morrels are scaulded in. Parboyl a sweetbread, put in Morrels, Palets, coxcombs, stir in a little Butter, to make the sauce of a proper thickness.

HAM PIE

THIS recipe, among others, was supplied to Mrs Acworth by Mr Andrews. Whoever he was, his recipe is a classic such as was to be found, with variations, in the repertoire of most eighteenth-century cooks and in virtually all printed cookery books during the century. The pie would be cooked in the special pastry reserved for raised pies (see p. 75), and embellished with pastry cut-outs, perhaps using the little parchment patterns found loose in Mrs Acworth's book. At a dinner party it might have been one of the three or four main dishes set out for the first course. For everyday fare it would have been kept in the larder and sliced for luncheon or supper snacks. Hannah Glasse in *The Art of Cookery made Plain and Easy* remarked that a fresh ham would not be so tender as one that had been boiled the day before. She always served her boiled ham one day and then used the remains of it to make ham pie the next.

Ragout was a mixture added to pies at the end of their cooking, but in this recipe it can equally well be added to the pie before it first goes into the oven. Mrs Acworth clearly liked the ragout in Mr Andrews's recipe as a dish by itself, perhaps as a light supper dish when she was not entertaining company. As in the recipe for Pottage on p. 34, we have substituted lamb's tongues for palates and small pieces of bacon for cocks' combs.

a piece of gammon, smoked or unsmoked, weighing about 2½ lbs
(1.15 kg)
about 1 teaspoon each of vinegar and brown sugar
1 or 2 bay leaves
4 small lambs' tongues
salt
1 large or 2 small onions
about 5 cloves
8 oz (225 g) lambs' sweetbreads
4 oz (115 g) mushrooms
about 1 oz (30 g, 1 tablespoon) butter
2 slices of bacon
about 1 tablespoon flour
salt, pepper, extra bay leaves, basil, thyme and parsley
suet crust pastry, or Pastry for Raised Pies (see p. 75) using 1 lb
(450 g, 3 cups and 1 tablespoon) flour

If the gammon is smoked, soak it for about 4 hours before cooking. Put it in a large pan, just cover with water, and add a dash of wine vinegar, a teaspoonful of brown sugar, and one or two bay leaves. Bring to the boil, then reduce the heat and leave it to simmer until it is cooked (about 1½ hours). Remove the skin and all or most of the fat and cut the meat into cubes. Meanwhile, cook the tongues in salted water with the onion(s) stuck with cloves, a bunch of parsley and 3 or 4 bay leaves, until they are tender (about 1½ hours). Keep the stock, remove the tongues and trim off the skin and gristle. Cut them into small pieces like the ham. While the ham and tongues are cooking, soak the sweetbreads for at least 2 hours in cold water with a dash of lemon juice or vinegar. Put them in a pan with fresh salted water, bring them to the boil and cook for 2 minutes. Drain, cool and trim the sweetbreads and cut them into small dice. Wash and slice the mushrooms. To make the ragout, lightly fry the chopped sweetbreads and slices of bacon in a little butter, sprinkle flour over them and make a sauce using the remainder of the tongue stock. Stir in the chopped tongues, finely chopped basil, thyme and parsley. Adjust the seasoning to taste, remembering that the ham itself will be quite salty. Allow the mixture to cool slightly, then place the ham and ragout in a deep pie dish and cover with a suet pastry crust. Alternatively, make a raised pie case with the pastry described on p. 75 and fill it with the ham and ragout. Cover this with a pastry lid. Whichever pastry is used, bake for 40 minutes in an oven preheated to gas mark 3 (325°F, 170°C).

PIGEONS IN SCOLLOP SHELLS Take six young Pigeons scald &
draw ym, truss ye feet inside ye Body, don't cut of ye heads, blanch & pick ym
clean yn put ym a stewing in a small pot with slices of Bacon, & Lemmon,
pepper, salt, Sweet herbs, & a Glass of White Wine. Make a small rague with
sweetbreads of Veal, Champignons, Truffles. Divide this Rague into 3
Saucepans, one with a white sauce another with cray fish Cullice & tayles,
Cockcombs, & ye other with Cullice of Ham. Yn take 6 shells, silver or china.
Round each make a small border of Paste as neat as possible, rub it over with
Egg & let it be baked, yn put ye shells in ye Dish, take ye Pidgeon, put of
they're seasoning & put 2 in each shell. Ye Cullices being well season'd, put one
sort in each shell & ye 3 different sauces, ye one yth brown ye other white &
other Red seperate in each shell. Ye little bills to be seen as peeping out of
ye shell.

PIGEONS IN SCALLOP SHELLS

THIS recipe was given to Mrs Acworth by a friend. Cullis was a rich
stock and ragout, in Mrs Acworth's usage, a thick sauce based on a
cullis, with pieces of meat in it. Ragout was commonly added to meat
pies near to the end of the cooking time, as in Mr Andrews's recipe for a
Ham Pie (p. 70). This particular dish must have excited great admiration
in its original version, with the pigeons' heads peeping out from beneath
variously coloured sauces, atop silver scallop shells. These days few of us
would have the stomach for cooked heads and perhaps fewer still the
time to concoct three complex sauces while also preparing vegetables
and other courses. The version which follows is simplified, but it would
be fun to try the full original for a grand occasion one day.

6 pigeons
about 1 tablespoon cooking oil
6 slices of bacon
1 lemon
a bunch of herbs including parsley, sage, thyme and a bay leaf
salt and pepper
8 fl oz (225 ml, 1 cup) dry white wine
1 lb (450 g) calves' sweetbreads, soaked in cold water with a dash
of lemon juice for 2 hours
2 tablespoons flour
4 oz (115 g) mushrooms
2 oz (60 g, $\frac{1}{4}$ cup) butter
10 fl oz (280 ml, 1$\frac{1}{4}$ cups) veal or chicken stock
extra parsley for decoration

Brown the pigeons lightly in a little oil in the bottom of the stewing pan
or casserole in which they are to cook, add the bacon cut into small strips,

the rind of the lemon, finely sliced, the bunch of herbs and a little pepper and salt. Pour the wine over all of these, bring it rapidly to the boil, and place the casserole in the oven at gas mark 3 (325°F, 170°C) to cook for about 40 minutes. While the pigeons are cooking, blanch the sweetbreads in boiling water for 2 minutes. Trim off the membranes and threads of fat, slice them about ½ inch (1 cm) thick, and fry gently in a little butter. When the sweetbreads are tender, sprinkle a little flour over them and make a sauce using the veal or chicken stock. Do not allow the butter or flour to brown, as this will colour the sauce, which should remain as white as possible. When the pigeons are cooked, leave the sweetbread sauce in a low oven to keep warm. Remove the pigeons on to a dish and keep them warm in the oven too. Slice the mushrooms thinly and fry them in a little butter, sprinkling them with flour when they are just beginning to soften. Make a sauce using the juices from the pigeons. Now cut the pigeons in halves, arrange them on scallop shells or in some other small dishes, covering the halves alternately with the sweetbread and mushroom sauces. Sprinkle a little parsley over them and serve.

TO DRESS A HARE Take the liver of the hare & boyle it & when cold chop it in with a little sweet Marioram, Lemmon peal, pasley, tybme, one Anchovy. Chop all the above together very fine then season it with pepper, salt & Nuttmegs. Then work it up with a peace of butter & putt it into the belly of the Hare, Basting the Hare with Salt and water for a Quarter of an Hour. Then putt in some Milk into the Driping pan & bast it offten with that & lett a Bunch of sweet yerbs Lay in your pan & sprinkle the Hair offten with that. Putt in one pint of Creem & milk, some of the milk in the pan with it, and take some of the pudding out of the belly & mix it with the sauce & searve it up.

HARE WITH CREAM SAUCE

Hare was a delicacy even in prehistoric times, and recipes for it are to be found in some of the earliest manuals of cookery. In English cooking, 'jugged' hare was particularly popular. This meant placing the hare in a jug inside a cauldron of water (in which other dishes might be cooking at the same time). Inside its jug, the hare cooked in its own juices with herbs and an onion. Contemporary printed cookery books also included recipes for roasted hare and some (including Hannah Glasse) used milk, but Mrs Acworth's recipe is not quite like any of them. It is not complicated to make, and involves no extravagant ingredients, but the blend of flavours is just right, with the milk and cream softening the strong gamy flavour of the hare, and the herbs adding interest. Part of the secret lies in frequent basting and long cooking, which makes the hare beautifully tender.

1 whole hare, including the liver
1 teaspoon each of dried marjoram, parsley and thyme, or 2
teaspoons each of fresh herbs
grated zest of ½ a lemon
2 anchovy fillets
salt and pepper
a bunch of herbs including thyme, parsley and bay leaf
½ nutmeg
16 fl oz (450 ml, 2 cups or 1 US pt) water
8 fl oz (225 ml, 1 cup) milk
1 oz (30 g, 1 tablespoon) butter or margarine
1 oz (30 g, 1 tablespoon) flour
8 fl oz (225 ml, 1 cup) single (light) cream
parsley and lemon slices to garnish

Barely cover the liver of the hare in a little cold water in a small pan and bring it gently to the boil. Reduce the heat and allow it to simmer until cooked. Mince the liver or mash it well in a bowl with a fork and add the herbs, lemon zest, finely chopped anchovy and a pinch of salt and pepper. Wash the hare well, discard any other giblets and put it in a deep roasting pan or casserole. Put the liver and herb mixture in the stomach cavity. Pour water and about a tablespoon of coarse sea salt over the hare, add a bunch of herbs and some grated nutmeg, and put it in the oven, uncovered, to cook at gas mark 5 (375°F, 190°C) for 15 minutes. Half-way through that time, remove the hare from the oven, baste it with the water and turn it over before replacing it in the oven. After 15 minutes' cooking, remove it again and pour in the milk, basting it again. This time return the pan to the oven well covered with a lid or sheet of cooking foil. After another 15 minutes, baste the hare again, turn it over, return it to the oven and reduce the heat to gas mark 3 (325°F, 170°C). It should cook for a further 3 hours, during which time it should be basted and turned several times. Always return it to the oven well covered, so that it does not become dry. When the hare is tender, lift it on to a meat dish, carve it into portions and return it to a very low oven, covered with foil, to keep warm. Pour the cream into the roasting dish and stir all the liquid together well, scraping the sides and bottom to get all the flavour, before pouring it into a saucepan. Remove the bunch of herbs and bring the liquid rapidly to the boil. Pour some of it over the hare and garnish the dish with parsley and slices of lemon. Serve the remainder of the sauce separately.

TO MAKE PAST FOR STANDING PYES Take 14 pound of flower, put to it 4 yolks of Egs, then make your Liquor boyl & putt in two pound of fresh Butter, a quarter of a pound of clarified Suet, then make your past stiff.

PASTRY FOR RAISED PIES

THE quantities given here suggest either that the Acworths entertained on a massive scale, or that they and their household ate pie for a week at a time. We have reduced the quantities to approximately one seventh, producing enough pastry to line and cover two 8 inch (20 cm) oval pie moulds or to make two pies using a 7 inch (18 cm) diameter cake tin, each pie producing four to six hearty helpings. The art of making pastry for pies is beautifully described in Elizabeth Ayrton's *The Cookery of England*. Mrs Acworth's recipe, though it is a good version of the sort of pastry that was probably most widely used in her day, is but one of several possibilities for making delicious pies.

2 lbs (900 g, 6¼ cups) plain wheatmeal flour
1 teaspoon salt
3 oz (85 g, ¾ cup) shredded suet (kidney fat)
5 oz (140 g, ½ cup plus 1 tablespoon) butter or margarine
2 fl oz (60 ml, ¼ cup) water, or a little more if necessary
1 small egg

Sift the flour and salt into a large mixing bowl or into the bowl of a food processor. Melt together the suet, butter or margarine and water and pour these hot into the flour, along with the yolk of the egg. Knead until the dough is soft and malleable, then roll it out immediately on a floured board or table until it is about ¼ inch (5 mm) thick. If you have a raised pie mould, grease it and line it with the dough, reserving enough to make the lid and to decorate this with cut-out leaves, flowers or what you will. Alternatively, use a round cake tin to make the shape of the pie, rolling out the pastry to a circle, standing the tin in the centre and moulding the dough up around the sides. When you have done this, remove the tin gently from inside the dough, and you then have a pie shell ready for filling and covering with a lid made from some of the extra dough. Brush the top of the pie with a little of the white of the egg, lightly beaten on a saucer. Bake the filled pie in a moderate to hot oven for at least 30 minutes, or longer if the recipe requires.

CHAPTER FOUR

VEGETABLES
AND PICKLES

Artichoke Pie
Potted Asparagus
Pickled Red Cabbage
Stewed Cucumbers
Pickled Kidney Beans
Pickled French Beans
Pickled Onions
Pickled Mushrooms
Stewed Mushrooms

Asparagus for Potted Asparagus; Pickled Red and White Kidney Beans; Stewed Mushrooms

THE range of vegetables available to Mrs Acworth from her garden or local market was considerable: artichokes, asparagus, beans, red cabbage, carrots, celery, cucumbers, lettuce, mushrooms, onions, peas, sorrel, spinach and turnips to name only a few that she mentions in her manuscript. Since she lived close to the market gardens west of London she must have had plentiful supplies of cheap vegetables in season. She used them habitually in mixed meat dishes and as a garnish, but had very few recipes for vegetables cooked on their own. We may assume that she simply boiled vegetables in salted water and thus did not think formal recipes were necessary. Whether she overcooked them, as Hannah Glasse complained that so many cooks did, we cannot tell. Overcooked or not, we may also assume that in this 'golden age' of butter cookery, she added butter to them. Melted butter was ever-present with vegetables on the tables of the rich in the eighteenth century.

Mrs Acworth's vegetables often appear more imaginatively in her soups, meat and game dishes: lettuce and celery in her Gravy Soup, artichokes and mushrooms with Scotch Collops. In many such dishes, she probably drew on her stock of pickles, for which there are many recipes in her cookery book. Some are unusual, such as pickled samphire and pickled melons. Others, such as pickled onions, red cabbage and mushrooms are still widely eaten today by those with a taste for vinegar. They certainly served Mrs Acworth's needs. Eaten as a salad or as a table relish with cold meats, or added to made dishes of meat, game and fish during their preparation, they were invaluable during the winter months when so many vegetables were unobtainable. Pickles were a reliable ally in her kitchen and a hedge against adversity.

Some of her pickle recipes were provided by her friend Betty Edmonds who, it would seem, had copied them out of Eliza Smith's *The Compleat Housewife*. Hannah Glasse gave sound rules for pickling in *The Art of Cookery*. She insisted that stone jars must be used for all vegetables pickled hot, and earthenware never used because vinegar and salt would penetrate it. 'Be sure never to put your Hands in to take Pickles out,' she added, 'it will soon spoil it. The best Way is to every Pot, tye a wooden Spoon full of little Holes, to take the Pickles out with.' Others warned against the common practice of cooking pickles in copper pans to turn them green. This may be what Mrs Acworth did with her pickled kidney beans, but it was a dangerous practice because the resulting liquid was poisonous.

To SEASON A HARTICHOAK PYE Boyl them and take away the bottoms. Cut them in thin slices. Season them with Cinamon, Nutmeg, Shugger and rose water, Lemon peal in Bates shred fine. Put in good store of Marrow, fill the pye & bake it moderately.

ARTICHOKE PIE

THIS well-flavoured pie would have been served alongside meats and fish dishes, probably in the second course of a dinner, as one of the side dishes. For modern taste it belongs firmly with the dessert course. It is certainly an interesting way with artichokes. If globe artichokes and the time to fiddle about with them are in short supply, Jerusalem artichokes, which are quite unrelated botanically but taste very similar, make a remarkably good substitute. We have not found that artichoke hearts from a tin work so well, because their texture does not blend well into a pie. The butter in our version substitutes for marrow, which would have supplied the original richness of this dish.

12 globe or Jerusalem artichokes
shortcrust pastry made with 10 oz (280 g, 2 cups) flour
1 teaspoon ground cinnamon
½ nutmeg
2 tablespoons rose-water
grated zest of 1 lemon
2 oz (60 g, scant ⅓ cup) granulated sugar
2 oz (60 g, ¼ cup) butter
cream, to serve

If you are using globe artichokes, boil them in unsalted water for about 30 minutes. Remove the solid bottoms just above the stems, and discard the hairy choke and the leaves. Cut the bottoms into thin slices. If you are using Jerusalem artichokes, peel them well, plunge them into boiling, unsalted water and boil them for about 20 minutes, until they are soft but still firm. Slice them thinly. Line a deep flan dish with pastry and put in half of the artichoke slices. Sprinkle the cinnamon, grated nutmeg, rose-water, grated lemon zest and most of the sugar over them, then add the remaining slices. Sprinkle these with the rest of the sugar, and the butter cut into little dice. Cover with a pastry lid, brush lightly with beaten egg or milk to glaze it and bake at gas mark 4 (350°F, 180°C) for about 50 minutes. Serve hot, with cream.

To KEEP ASPARAGRASS ALL THE YEAR Parboyl it very little and put into Clarify'd butter. Cover it and when ye butter is Cold cover it with leather and Set it under Ground.

POTTED ASPARAGUS

Asparagus was one of the vegetables which reached England in the sixteenth century from the Continent. This recipe is very much in line with the way the dish has been prepared since Elizabethan times. Given that asparagus is now available for much of the year, either imported, tinned or frozen, there is less need for us to store it for later consumption. Moreover, it is best eaten fresh. This version, however, provides a pleasant surprise as the starter at a winter dinner party or for a quick, delicious snack. Serve it with wholemeal bread and butter.

2 lb (900 g) fresh asparagus
4 oz (115 g, ½ cup) butter

Lightly wash the asparagus and trim the stalks to be all about the same length. Tie them into two or three bundles. Stand them in a saucepan tall enough for you to cover them with the lid and pour in enough water to come about half-way up the stalks. Remove the asparagus while you bring the water to the boil, then plunge the bundles into the boiling water, cover, and allow to cook over a moderate heat until the stalks begin to feel soft when prodded gently with a knife. (They should not be as tender as if you were going to serve the asparagus straight away.) This may take anything from just under 10 minutes to nearly 30, depending on the thickness and type of asparagus: it is better to err on the side of undercooking. Take the asparagus out of the saucepan and lay it gently on a cloth to drain. When it has cooled, put it in a preserving jar and pour boiling butter over it. The butter should cover the tips of the asparagus. Seal the jar well and keep it in a cool place. We have not tried keeping potted asparagus for a year, but it is quite reliable after three months.

TO PICKELL RED CABBAGE Take a Close red cabage & Cutt it in Quarters. Make your pickells of the best White Wine Vinigar & Clarit, Spices & Salt. Boyle in it some Slices of beat root & when it boyles putt into it your Cabage & lett it boyle 2 minutes & putt it into a pott & when Cold Tye it downe very Close so keep it for Use.

PICKLED RED CABBAGE

R ED cabbage, grown in most English gardens in the eighteenth century, was much loved, especially as a pickle. Most people today either love the flavour or detest it. Jane Grigson, no friend to the dish, laments in her *Vegetable Book* that 'this extraordinary taste . . . darkened many high teas of [her] childhood'. This recipe is the same as one in Eliza Smith's *The Compleat Housewife* and is interesting for its use of beetroot, which added colour to a salad.

1 small red cabbage weighing about 1 lb (450 g)
8 fl oz (225 ml, 1 cup) white wine vinegar
12 fl oz (340 ml, 1½ cups) red wine
2 cloves of garlic
6 cloves
1 teaspoon salt
½ teaspoon pepper
4 oz (115 g) peeled beetroot

Cut the red cabbage into quarters, removing the outer leaves and stalks. Bring your pickle, made of white wine vinegar, red wine, and spices to the boil. (You may wish to substitute nutmeg or allspice for the garlic and cloves.) Slice the beetroot and add it to the pickle. When this comes to the boil add the red cabbage and let it boil for 2 minutes. When cool, seal in a sterilized pickle jar. Store for several days before eating but eat within a month, as cabbage loses its crispness.

TO STEW CUCUMBERS Pear your Cucumbers & cutt them in thick peaces. Putt a peace of butter as big as a walnut into your stewpan & when it is hot put your cucumbers in and lett them fry brown with a small oynon or two. When they are browne flower them but not before they are fryd browne. Then putt some good gravy pepper & salt & a little elder vinigar or else a little common vinigar but be shure you scum it well as they stew. When they are thick a nouf take the oynon out and searve them up hott.

STEWED CUCUMBERS

M R Andrews supplied several of the recipes interleaved in Mrs Acworth's book, notably the Ham Pie on page 70. This simple recipe is particularly good if you happen to have some well-flavoured veal or turkey stock for the sauce. The delicate flavour of the cucumbers goes well with chicken or veal, or as a foil to ham.

1 lb (450 g) cucumbers or gherkins
2 small onions
2 oz (60 g, $\frac{1}{4}$ cup) butter
about 1 tablespoon flour
salt and pepper
1 tablespoon wine vinegar
about 4 fl oz (115 ml, $\frac{1}{2}$ cup) stock

Peel the cucumber(s), slice them about an inch (2.5 cm) thick and dice the onions. Fry in butter till both sides of the cucumber slices are brown, sprinkle flour, salt and pepper over them and then stir in the liquid. Allow the sauce to thicken, then serve. These quantities will serve four to six people.

To PICKLE KIDNEY BEANS Take some of ye smallest Kidney Beans that is White, Lay 'em in Water and salt 3 Days and 3 Nights then boyle 'em in White Wine Vinigar and Water, of each a little quantity. Lett 'em boyle but a short time, put in a small quantity of roachs allom. Cover 'em as Close as possable you can. Past Downe ye cover of your pot. Keepe some embers under your pot and do not open it for 3 or 4 hours. If you find they are not greene, give 'em a warme or two and cover 'em Downe for 2 or 3 hours more. Let 'em lye in ye same liquor they were Boyl'd in then take of White Wine and White Wine Vinigar an Equal quantity, two Rases of Ginger cutt into small peices, Some Large Mace and Cloves and a llttle bay salt. Lett this boyl for half a quarter of an hour then putt it into the vessell which you intend to keepe ye Beanes in. Lett it stand till it is could then take ye Beanes out of ye Liquor and put 'em in ye pickle.

PICKLED KIDNEY BEANS

This recipe can be made with either white or red kidney beans, and looks rather good with a mixture of both. It was probably served as a side dish alongside the main meat dishes of the first course. The alum in the recipe is unusual, and having used it with caution we have been unable to discover that it makes much difference.

6 oz (170 g, 1 cup) dried kidney beans
water to cover
2 tablespoons sea salt
$\frac{1}{2}$ pint (280 ml, 1$\frac{1}{4}$ cups) each of water and white wine vinegar
FOR THE PICKLE:
$\frac{1}{2}$ pint (280 ml, 1$\frac{1}{4}$ cups) each of wine vinegar and white wine
$\frac{1}{2}$ teaspoon each of ground cloves, ground mace and sea salt
about 1 tablespoon grated fresh ginger

Soak the beans for three days and nights in enough water to cover them well, stirred with about 2 tablespoons of sea salt. Skim off the white scum which rises to the surface, strain off the water and place the beans in a pan with the water and wine vinegar, adding equal quantities of each, if necessary, to cover the beans. Bring them to the boil and allow to boil briskly for at least 20 minutes, skimming off any further scum. Cover the saucepan and leave it over a low heat for three hours without lifting the lid. By this time the liquid will be nearly all absorbed. Set the beans to one side and prepare the pickle by boiling together all the ingredients briskly for about 5 minutes. Pour the liquid into clean, warm, sterilized jars and leave it to cool. When it is quite cold, strain any liquid from the beans and pour them into the jars and seal them well. The quantities given here will fill about two 1 lb (450 g) jam or preserving jars.

To PICKELL CUCUMBERS, FRENCH BEANS OR PUS-LAN STALKS Gather them on a dry day and putt them into a Earthen pan and putt water & salt to them Scalding hott. Cover them down Very Close that no Steem Comes from them. Do this 6 or 7 mornings together and they will be Green. The last time then throw in a Little peace of Allam then Make a pickell for them of rape & Vinigar, boyle in whole pepper, Cloves, Mace & Ginger, a Little Green dell. When it boyles throw the things you pickell in. Do but scald them & take them out again and putt them in Again when the pickell is Cold.

PICKLED FRENCH (GREEN) BEANS

THIS is something of a catch-all pickle recipe, which Mrs Acworth received from a Mr Silly. Purslane, spelled puslan in the recipe, is a succulent herb used in salads in the eighteenth century but which is now difficult to find except in seedmen's catalogues. Various French beans, native to America but introduced to England from France, were highly regarded for their flavour. Using small French green beans we have reduced the amount of preparation required. We have also substituted white wine for rape, which was the refuse of grapes after wine-making. Mrs Acworth, of course, would have had plenty of rape available from her home-made wines.

1 lb (450 g) French (green) beans
2 tablespoons sea salt
12 fl oz (340 ml, 1½ cups) white wine
12 fl oz (340 ml, 1½ cups) white wine vinegar
12 peppercorns
6 cloves
½ teaspoon each of mace, ground ginger and dill seed

Clean, top and tail your beans and put them in a saucepan. Scald them with salted boiling water, cover the saucepan and let them stand until cool, preferably overnight. Repeat this procedure two or three times, depending on the tenderness required. The smaller the beans the more quickly they become tender. Make your pickle of white wine, white wine vinegar, peppercorns, cloves, mace, ginger and dill seed and bring it to the boil. Add the beans but after scalding them take them out with a spoon. Do not boil the pickle any longer than necessary. When it has cooled pour it into a sterilized jar and put the beans in. They should stand for a week before using and will keep for several months after opening.

TO PICKELL SMALL OINIONS Take young White Oinions as big as your fingir top, peal them and putt them into salt and water and Lett them Stand two days. Shifting the water once, then drane them in a Cloath. Boyle the best White Wine Vinigar with Spices and Salt to your Tast, and when it is Cold pour it to them and Tye it downe close with a bladder.

PICKLED ONIONS

Pᴵᴄᴷᴸᴱᴰ onions were often served as a simple salad in the winter or provided a garnish for meat and fish dishes. In many recipes of the period they are boiled, but in this one, which also appears in Eliza Smith's *The Compleat Housewife*, they are eaten raw, or used by Mrs Acworth to flavour soups, pottages or stews. Mace, ginger and bay leaves were commonly used in recipes for pickled onions.

1 lb (450 g) small onions
½ teaspoon salt
16 fl oz (450 ml, 2 cups or 1 US pint) white wine vinegar
1 teaspoon mace
1 teaspoon ground ginger
3–4 bay leaves
½ teaspoon ground pepper

Put the peeled onions in salted water, let them stand for two days and then drain them. Boil the vinegar containing mace, ground ginger, bay leaves, pepper and an extra pinch of salt. When cold add it to the onions and store in a sterilized pickle jar. Allow to mature for several weeks. They will keep for three months.

TO PICKEL MUSHROOMS Take them of a nights Growth, peel them on both sides and put water and Salt to them all night. The next morning throw them into water and Salt Scalding hot over the fier do but just Scald them and Take them out Again and Lay them to Cool. Then putt them into a Great Glass and putt to them whole Cloves, Mace, Ginger and pepper and then fill up the Glass with white wine and white wine Vinigar. Cover them close and keep them Covered for use.

PICKLED MUSHROOMS

THIS recipe, which may have been borrowed from Eliza Smith's *The Compleat Housewife*, uses a mixture of white wine and white wine vinegar, but the precise quantity of each is not given. If we have erred in interpretation it is on the side of the wine, for our taste for vinegar is less marked than Mrs Acworth's. As with many other pickles, these mushrooms may be eaten by themselves or used to garnish other dishes. Kept in store they also provide a ready addition to sauces or stews.

1 lb (450 g) fresh button mushrooms
salt to taste
6 cloves
1 teaspoon mace
1 teaspoon ground ginger
½ teaspoon ground pepper
16 fl oz (450 ml, 2 cups or 1 US pint) dry white wine
2 fl oz (60 ml, ¼ cup) white wine vinegar

Soak the mushrooms in salted water. The next day put them in boiling salted water briefly, just to scald them, then remove and dry. Place them in a sterilized pickle or preserving jar and add the cloves, mace, ginger, pepper, wine and white wine vinegar. There should be enough liquid to cover the mushrooms. They will keep for several weeks once opened.

To Stew Mushrooms Take mushrooms and when you have pilled and washed them Cleane put them into a Dry Dish over coales till ye heat hath drawne out ye Liquor from them. Then pour out there owne Liquor from them and put to them a good Quantity of Gravey.

STEWED MUSHROOMS

M RS Acworth used mushrooms, morels and truffles in her cookery, but this is her only recipe for mushrooms cooked separately. They would have been flat field mushrooms, probably freshly picked on the day they were cooked.

mushrooms
a well-flavoured beef stock

Put the wiped mushrooms in an ovenproof dish and cook them with whatever else is in the oven until they have turned black inside and the juice has run out of them. Pour off the juice (which could be kept for adding to soup) and serve them covered with beef stock.

CHAPTER FIVE

BREADS, CAKES
AND PASTRIES

Wigs
Manchet
Griddle Cakes
Seed Cake
Orange Cake
Sweetmeat Cake
A 'Plain' Cake
Rachel Manaton's Plum Cake
Irish Plum Cake
An Excellent Fruit Cake
Plain Icing
Little Cakes
Gingerbread
Macaroons
Jumbles

Irish Plum Cake; Jumble; Manchet; Gingerbread; Macaroon

I T is the baking recipes that often tell us most about cooking equipment and methods of the past. Mrs Acworth's recipes for bread and cakes show that she almost certainly had a brick or clay oven built into the wall beside her kitchen fire, and probably also a 'backstone' on which to bake griddle cakes at the back of the fire, where the embers would keep the stone hot. Several of her recipes, like the one for Manchet, refer to the oven being 'stopt up'. This meant that the fuel to heat the oven, which might have been furze or twigs or in London more probably coal, would burn quickly for one or two hours with the oven door open to let out the smoke. The early morning, when this was happening, must have been an unpleasant time for the kitchen staff.

When the oven was white hot, the ashes would be cleaned out and loaves and cakes put in, either standing on the floor of the oven or on griddles or baking trays. The door could then be closed and the oven would retain most of its heat for several hours, only gradually cooling down to the more moderate temperature suitable for cooking tarts and cheesecakes. It was an important part of the art of cooking to know how to time one's baking, for if the oven was too hot or had cooled too fast, a whole batch of cakes, bread and pies could be spoiled.

The provident housewife would judge the sizes of her loaves and cakes to a nicety in order to take advantage of the cooking time and space available to her. Most of Mrs Acworth's cakes were enormous, though she also produced batches of little cakes or buns. The vast sweetmeat cake, for example, used eight pounds of flour and must have called for all the elbow grease that one sturdy kitchen maid or boy could muster to knead the dough. Baked for only two hours, it would have gone into the oven with the bread, when the heat was at its highest, and it would have needed Mrs Acworth's largest hoop to bake it. Hoops for baking cakes were made of wood or tin. They stood on iron or tin baking trays, sometimes on a layer of brown paper to prevent a soft dough from running out or burning at the bottom. More liquid cake mixtures were cooked in pans and there were pie moulds for raised or standing pies and patty pans for tarts and cheesecakes.

Many housewives, especially in the country, had their own bake-houses. In other households it was common to send pies and cakes, suitably marked with the owner's initial, to be cooked at a public bakery. Mrs Acworth probably sent some of her pies out in this way, for the instruction to send a dish out to the bakehouse appears in several of her recipes. The bakery of Tobias Payne (mentioned in the 1749 poll book) was only a few steps away in Marsham Street. There may have been days when her own oven was too full of cakes and tarts to accommodate the pies as well. To judge from her cookery book it would seldom have been full of bread, for she gives few bread recipes, though she clearly used it in considerable quantities.

The bread recipes which do appear in this book are for delicacies now rare in English cooking. They are well worth reviving. The spicy, wedge-shaped Wigs would have been eaten at breakfast time, perhaps with a cup of hot chocolate, tea or coffee. Or they might make a snack with a piece of cheese. The so-called 'oatcakes', baked on a backstone, may have been intended for breakfast too. They also go well with cheese. Manchet was a white bread of fine quality, used by Mrs Acworth as synonymous with French bread. The word had been used to denote small, fine white loaves, probably enriched with butter and eggs, from the late fifteenth century at least, supplanting 'paynedemayn', which was mentioned in Chaucer. The history of manchets and French bread is traced in fascinating detail in Elizabeth David's *English Bread and Yeast Cookery*. Mrs David also follows the development of yeast as a leaven from the days of the ancient Egyptians onwards. Liquid 'ale yeast' procured from breweries or left over from home brewing had been used as a leaven for bread in France and England for about a century before Margaretta Acworth set up house. It is invariably ale yeast that she recommends, but she probably washed it very carefully several times and soaked it overnight, to reduce its bitterness. We have substituted dried yeast, a modern convenience which almost certainly produces a less beery flavour than the original. We also use a combination of stone-ground wheatmeal flour, i.e. flour with 85 per cent of the bran and wheatgerm left in, with strong white bread flour. This comes close, we hope, to the sort of texture that Mrs Acworth would have expected from her 'white' flour. For the oatcakes, wholemeal flour works best.

Mrs Acworth's cakes covered a wide range. She is likely to have partaken in the relatively new fashion of serving cakes and tea to afternoon callers, probably at three or four, before Abraham Acworth returned from the government offices. Those who liked cake would have called often. We have selected from a quantity of recipes two based on yeast, the Sweetmeat Cake and a Seed Cake, both of which could have derived from earlier centuries. They have a firm, bread-like consistency and can be eaten with butter, though both are excellent without it.

During the eighteenth century cooks made increasing use of eggs as raising agents in preference to yeast, and most of Mrs Acworth's cake recipes follow this trend. We have not included any of the several recipes for pound cake, which are similar to numerous published versions. But we could not resist the recipe for 'Plain' Cake which shows the fashion for eggs in cake-baking carried to extreme. Having found that in most of Mrs Acworth's recipes she used fairly small eggs, corresponding to the modern European size 4, we incautiously used her own proportions in this case. The cake rose spectacularly as it cooked, holding out the promise of feather-light mouthfuls. The brandy, which we had also used in Mrs Acworth's proportions, smelled delicious. Within five minutes of being removed from the oven, the centre of our beautiful tall cake plummeted, leaving a hole in the middle and a rather solid mass on the outside. We tried again, cooking it longer and slower, but the cake rose and descended as precipitately as before. Only at the third attempt and getting close to the bottom of the brandy bottle did we reduce the quantity of eggs and succeed in producing a good, if far from 'plain' cake. Perhaps Mrs Acworth never actually cooked this recipe.

Her fruit cakes are much closer to modern versions and are so good that we have included three of them. Rachel Manaton's Plum Cake recipe deserves particular attention for the insight it gives us into cooking methods. It took half an hour to whip the egg whites to a 'crud' or crust. Everything was to be well beaten and mixed together quickly, with the fruit warmed before it was added. This cake seems to have started its baking in an open oven, for it was to be covered with a sheet of paper after it had risen, before the oven was stopped up. After it had cooled it was iced, without any marzipan under the icing, and returned to a cool oven for the icing to dry. Probably meant for special occasions, it certainly makes an excellent Christmas cake.

Gingerbread, one of the best loved of traditional sweetmeats, was in a state of transition during the eighteenth century from the stiff, highly spiced versions of earlier centuries to the more cake-like modern version. Mrs Acworth had a recipe using large quantities of molasses and spices. This produced a scorching, chewy concoction which explains one of the best-known street cries of mid-Georgian London, that of the celebrated, fancifully dressed Tiddy Diddy Doll: 'Here's your nice gingerbread, your spiced gingerbread, which will melt in your mouth like a red-hot brickbat, and rumble in your inside like Punch in a wheelbarrow'. Mrs Acworth preferred her gingerbread with less spice, and we have followed her example.

To Make Wiggs Take 3 pound of ffine fflower, one pound of butter. Rub it all cold into ye fflower. Some Cloves and Mace, nutmeg, ginger, Salt, of each a quantity, ye yolks and Whites of 6 eggs, a pint of good Ale yeast, Warme milke as much as will make it into an indifferent soft paste. Worke it all together and set it before ye fire to Rise. When it is Risen worke in half a pound of caraway comfits. Put them on papers and bake them in a pretty quick oven.

WIGS

WIGS were a sort of spiced bun, known at least as far back as the fifteenth century and apparently universally popular in eighteenth-century England. Their name derives from a German or Flemish word meaning wedge. To addicts of modern spiced hot cross buns the flavour of Mrs Acworth's Wigs will be enticingly familiar.

about 12 oz (340 g, 2⅔ cups) wheatmeal flour
4 oz (115 g, scant 1 cup) strong white bread flour
1 teaspoon dried yeast
8 fl oz (225 ml, 1 cup) water
¼ teaspoon sugar
5 oz (140 g, ½ cup plus 1 tablespoon) butter or margarine
1 teaspoon each of salt and ground mace, ginger, nutmeg and cloves
1 tablespoon caraway seeds
1 tablespoon more of sugar
2 eggs
8 fl oz (225 ml, 1 cup) milk

Sift the flours together into a mixing bowl and leave it to stand in a warm place while you dissolve the yeast in the water, which you have heated to blood heat (98.6°F, 37°C) with ¼ teaspoon of sugar. Cut the butter or margarine into small pieces and rub it into the flour as you would for pastry, until the mixture is the consistency of fine breadcrumbs. Mix the other dry ingredients including the caraway seeds and extra sugar into the flour. Whisk the eggs, warm the milk to blood heat and when the yeast is frothy mix all the liquid ingredients together and stir them into the flour mixture. Knead the dough until it is soft, adding a little more warm milk or a little extra flour as necessary to make it smooth and malleable. Cover the bowl with a cloth and leave it in a warm place for the dough to rise for 30 minutes. Shape the dough into two round, flat buns, score them into wedges with a sharp knife, and bake on floured baking trays at gas mark 6 (400°F, 200°C) for about 30 minutes.

*T*O *MAKE MANCHET OR FRENCH BREAD Take ½ a peck of fine flower ye yolks of 3 Eggs and 2 Whites and ½ a pint of yeast 2 or 3 days old and some milke. Then take your milke and heat it so hott as to melt butter. Then put theirein a quarter of a pound of butter and Mix it with ye milke then take some of your butter and milke and mingle your flower with it then beate your eggs and yeast together and mix them with your flower then worke them well but it must not be to stiff when you have done this. If it be in the Winter it must be set by ye fire covered with a cloath that it may rise but if in summer let it stand a little while cover'd. Then you must have your oven very hott and mold it very Quick. Put it in ye oven and lett it bake for ½ an hour ye mouth of ye oven being stopt.*

MANCHET

MRS Acworth's recipe is similar to one printed in Eliza Smith's *Compleat Housewife* but not so rich. She also omits the instruction given both by Eliza Smith and by Hannah Glasse in another recipe, to 'rasp' or grate the crust after the loaf was baked. While the French usually kept the hard crusts of their loaves, using them sometimes in soup, the English discarded them or gave them to their animals. For modern taste, these loaves are good crust and all. They can be eaten straight away or reheated. They also make good toast and are ideal for serving, sliced and lightly fried in butter or olive oil, with some of the veal and poultry dishes. Strong white bread flour will produce a closely grained, rather crumbly loaf with a hard crust. A combination of wheatmeal (i.e. 85 per cent extraction) plain flour with just a little strong white bread flour probably comes closer to the colour and texture that Mrs Acworth would have recognized. Either version is good, and it is part of the fun of the recipe to experiment with different sorts of flour.

1 lb 9 oz (700 g, 5 cups) flour (strong white bread flour or a mixture
of 4 parts plain wheatmeal flour to 1 part strong white flour)
½ oz (15 g, 1 tablespoon) dried yeast
about ½ pint (250 ml, 1 cup) milk
2 oz (60 g, ¼ cup) butter
1 whole egg plus 1 egg white

Sift the flour into a mixing bowl and set it to one side. Warm half of the milk to blood heat (98.6°F, 37°C) and sprinkle the dried yeast over it. Leave this to stand for about 5 minutes or so, until the yeast froths. Warm the rest of the milk to the same temperature, add the butter and let it melt. Lightly beat the eggs in with the butter and milk mixture, combine this with the yeast and milk mixture and stir it all together into the flour. Knead the dough until it is smooth, adding a little more slightly warm milk if necessary, and leave it, covered with a cloth, in a warm place for about half an hour. Heat the oven to gas mark 6 (400°F, 200°C). Break the dough into 4 pieces and mould each one into an oval shape about 10 inches (25 cm) long. Place on a lightly floured baking tray, score each loaf down the middle with a knife and bake for 20 minutes. Turn the cooked loaves out on to a wire rack to cool.

OAT CAKES To one Quart of flower 4 eggs. Mix it well with 3 or 4 Spoonfulls of Yeast, a little salt. Wet it up with milk. Beat it up Very Light then Sett it half an Hour before the fier to rise, then roll them out on flower'd Cloath the Size of an Oatcake & Bake them on a Back on a Charcole fier.

GRIDDLE CAKES

Oatcakes, usually made with oatmeal and water, were a staple of the rural diet in the eighteenth century. Mrs Acworth's oatcakes, made without oatmeal, were biscuits to be eaten with jam or marmalade, or perhaps with cheese. 'Bake them on a Back' means that they were to be baked on the backstone or bakestone, a slate or griddle set on the bread oven adjacent to her principal fire.

1 lb (450 g, 3 cups plus 1 tablespoon) wholemeal flour
½ teaspoon salt
4 fl oz (115 ml, ½ cup) milk
2 teaspoons dried yeast
3 large or 4 small eggs

Sift the flour and salt into a bowl. Warm the milk to blood heat (98.6°F, 37°C), sprinkle the yeast over it and set it to one side until it froths. Then whisk the milk and yeast with the eggs in a measuring jug. There should be 8 fl oz (225 g, 1 cup) of liquid altogether. Pour this into the flour and knead it into the dough. Leave it in a warm place covered with a cloth for 30 minutes. Roll the dough out as thinly as you would for shortcrust pastry and use a pastry cutter or upturned wine glass to cut it into rounds. Cook them on a lightly greased griddle or in a heavy frying pan for about 10 minutes on each side.

A SEED CAKE Take 4 pound and ¼ of flower, 2 pound and a ½ of butter, a pint of Creame, a pint of ale yeast, 22 eggs Leaving out ½ the Whites, a quarter of a pint of Rose Water, 2 pound of Carraways, ½ an Ounce of Mace, a quarter of an ounce of Nutmeggs, ½ a pound of Loafe sugar finley beaten. Strow your sugar and spice amongst your flower, beate your Rose Water, Eggs and yeast together then runn them through a sive and let your Creame melt in a Tankard or flagon in a kettle of Water. Then mix it with ye flower and ye eggs and lett it stand by ye fire to Rise. When your oven is swept, strow in your carraways into your Cake and put it into ye Oven as quick as you cann. Let it stand an Hour and a Halfe.

SEED CAKE

THIS is a delicious, rather bread-like cake. Mrs Acworth might have eaten it at breakfast or at tea time. It is at its peak of perfection when still warm from the oven, sliced and spread with butter.

1 lb (450 g, 3 cups plus 1 tablespoon) flour
1 teaspoon each ground mace and nutmeg
6 oz (170 g, ¾ cup) each butter and margarine
2 oz (60 g, ¼ cup) granulated sugar
8 fl oz (225 ml, 1 cup) milk or single (light) cream
1 tablespoon dried yeast
3 whole eggs, plus 2 egg yolks
1 tablespoon rose-water
3 oz (85 g, 3 tablespoons) caraway seeds

Sift the flour, mace and nutmeg together into a large mixing bowl. Cut the butter and margarine into small pieces and rub them into the flour until you have the consistency of breadcrumbs (as though for shortcrust pastry). Stir in the sugar. Warm the cream or milk to blood heat (98.6°F, 37°C), sprinkle the yeast over it and leave it in a warm place until it froths (about 10 minutes). When the yeast is frothy, beat in the eggs and rose-water, and pour this mixture into the flour, butter and sugar mixture. Knead until they form a soft dough. Cover the bowl with a cloth and leave it in a warm place until the dough has approximately doubled in size (about 2 hours). Heat the oven to gas mark 5 (375°F, 190°C). Work the caraway seeds into the dough and put it into a greased cake tin with plenty of room for expansion – a deep tin of 9 inches (23 cm) diameter will do well. Bake for about an hour.

ORANGE CAKES Take the peal of 3 China Orringes par'd very thin, one pound of fine sugar. Beat them together with one pound of flower & a pound of fresh butter melted & lett it stand till cold. Then beat them together with ten eggs.

ORANGE CAKE

THIS is a firm but moist cake, good with a cup of tea or served as part of a dessert with a syllabub or cream. China oranges were sweet and juicy and could have been imported either from China or, since the late seventeenth century, from Portugal. They were to be distinguished from Seville oranges which were used then, as now, in marmalade or in other recipes that needed a sharper flavour.

8 oz (225 g, 1⅔ cups) plain flour
8 oz (225 g, just over 1 cup) granulated sugar
grated zest of 3 small or 1½ large oranges
4 oz (115 g, ½ cup) each of butter and soft margarine
5 small eggs

Sift the flour and sugar into a bowl. Add the orange zest and mix well. Melt the butter and margarine together and pour them into the bowl. Mix all these ingredients together to a smooth dough, and leave to stand until it is cold. Whisk the eggs until they are frothy, pour into the mixture and beat well. Pour the finished mixture immediately into a greased ring-shaped cake tin and bake for approximately 40 minutes at gas mark 4 (350°F, 180°C). Alternatively, cook it in bun tins for 20 minutes or in a round, solid-bottomed cake tin for up to 50 minutes: the mixture is too runny for a tin with a removable base.

A SWEETE MEATE CAKE Take eight pound of fflower and Rubb into it 3 pound of new butter. Put in 3 grated nutmegs and 3 pound of Carroway Comfitts. Put ¹/₂ the Comfitts into the fflower after the butter is rubbed in, then take 1 pint of Creame and a pint and a ¹/₂ of Ale yeast, 12 eggs keeping out 4 of ye Whites. Beate them very well then mix ye eggs and Creame very well together. Straine them, then add ¹/₂ a pint of sack, a quarter of an ounce of Carraway seeds, mix all these with the fflower then set it before ye ffire untill your Oven is hott. Cover it warme and stir it often. Then take ¹/₂ a pound of Cittorne and ¹/₂ a pound of Lemon and Orange, ¹/₂ a pound of Ringoo Rootes. Slice all these and put them with ye rest of your Comfitts, then put your Cake into the hoope but be sure your oven be ready before you mingle it up. Put it into ye oven as soon as it is in ye Hoope. 2 Hours bakes it. When it is Drawne ice it.

SWEETMEAT CAKE

Here is a festive cake for an adventurous cook. It is one of two recipes in Mrs Acworth's book which included the elusive 'Ringoo Rootes'. Their proper name is Eringo, and they were the candied roots of sea holly. They were long held to be an aphrodisiac, and Falstaff called for the sky to 'snow eringoes' in *The Merry Wives of Windsor*. Sad to relate, we have been unable to obtain even a whiff of the stuff and cannot report on its qualities. The caraway comfits substituted for sugar as well as adding flavour to the cake. In our version we have substituted ginger for Eringo and a proportion of sugar for the comfits. We have added a few glacé cherries and some candied angelica to please the eye, if not the palate, as the Eringo might have done. The quantities are reduced here to a quarter, which results in a large, solid cake of excellent flavour, to be eaten at tea or breakfast time in small slices.

2 lbs (900 g, 6¼ cups) flour
6 oz (170 g, ¾ cup) each butter and margarine
8 oz (225 g, just over 1 cup) granulated sugar
1 tablespoon caraway seeds
1 small nutmeg
4 fl oz (115 ml, ½ cup) single (light) cream or milk
2 fl oz (60 g, ¼ cup) sherry
½ oz (15 g, 1 tablespoon) dried yeast
2 eggs, plus 1 egg yolk
about 3 oz (85 g, ⅔ cup when chopped small) altogether of candied
angelica and glacé cherries
6 oz (170 g, 1½ cups) chopped mixed candied peel
3 oz (85 g, ⅔ cup) glacé ginger

Sift the flour into a bowl and rub in the butter and margarine until it is like breadcrumbs, as though you were making pastry. Add the sugar and caraway seeds, grate in the nutmeg and mix well. Warm the cream or milk and sherry together over a low heat until they reach approximately blood heat (98.6°F, 37°C). Sprinkle the yeast on to the surface and leave it in a warm place until it froths (about 10 minutes). Whisk the eggs thoroughly and add them to the yeast mixture. Whisk them again lightly and pour the whole mixture into the flour, fat and sugar mixture. Knead all well together until the dough is soft and malleable. Cover it with a cloth and leave it in a warm place for at least 30 minutes. Heat the oven and chop up the cherries and angelica. Mix them with the candied peel and ginger (which may also need chopping smaller). Mix all well in to the dough, then immediately put the whole mixture into a greased cake tin 10 inches (25 cm) square. Smooth the surface well, put the cake into the oven straight away and cook it for 1 hour at gas mark 5 (375°F, 190°C). After it has cooled, ice the cake using the recipe on p. 103.

PLANE CAKE Take one pound of Flower dry, one pound of sugar, one pound of butter beat up by hand. Mix these with one ounce of carraway seeds then beat well 12 Eggs, both whites and yolks. Pour it in by Degrees with a large glass of brandy. Mix them altogether a quarter of an hour then putt it in 2 small pans. Ad grated Lemmon. NB One hour bakes it.

A 'PLAIN' CAKE

HERE is a far from plain recipe for a quite unusual cake. The end result is moist and well flavoured, with a slightly marbled appearance when you cut into it.

8 oz (225 g, 1⅔ cups) flour
1 tablespoon caraway seeds
8 oz (225 g, just over 1 cup) granulated sugar
8 oz (225 g, 1 cup) butter
4 small eggs
grated zest of ½ a lemon
2 fl oz (60 ml, ¼ cup) brandy

Sift the flour and add the caraway seeds to it. Cream together the sugar and butter and then stir in the flour, or mix them together in a food processor. Whisk the eggs to a froth, add the grated lemon zest and brandy, and pour this mixture slowly into the other. Mix well until you have a smooth, thick batter. Pour this into a greased 6 inch (15 cm) cake tin and bake at gas mark 5 (375°F, 190°C) for about 1½ hours.

A RECEIPT TO MAKE A PLUM CAKE Beat four pound of Butter to Cream with your hand. Beat and sift two pound of fine (Dubel refine) sugar. Mix the sugar and butter well together, then take 4 pound of flower dry'd well, mix it with the Sugar & butter, then put in a pint of Sack, take eight eggs to each pound of Flower, the Yolks & Whites beaten separate. Whip the whites til they come to a Crud which will take half an hour. Mix the whites first with the other things and then the yolks. Then take four pound of currants after they are washd & pickd plump & dryd, then mix them hot, have ready a pound of Almonds blanchd & shaved longways very thin, and mix them with half an ounce of mace and as much nutmeg beat and sifted. Put in what Cittern you please. Have everything ready before you begin to mix, keep it beating till you put it into the Oven, and it must be beat up very high. Let it Bake three hours, put Brown paper at the Bottom of the hoop to keep it from running out, Butter your hoop well. After it is risen and Colourd cover it with a sheet of paper before the Oven is stopd up.

RACHEL MANATON'S PLUM CAKE

THE recipe for this light, moist plum cake, written in an elegant hand and better spelled than many of Mrs Acworth's own recipes, was kept tucked into the cookery book, even though at some stage Mrs Acworth copied it out as well, with her cousin's name beside it.

8 oz (225 g, 1 cup) each of butter and margarine
8 oz (225 g, 1¼ cups) moist brown or caster sugar
1 lb (450 g, 3 cups plus 1 tablespoon) flour
8 eggs, separated
1 lb (450 g, 3 cups) currants, or mixed currants, sultanas (white raisins) and raisins
4 oz (115 g, 1 cup) mixed candied peel
4 oz (115 g, 1 cup) blanched, sliced almonds
1 teaspoon mace
1 small or ½ large nutmeg
4 fl oz (115 ml, ½ cup) dry or medium-dry sherry

Mix together the butter and margarine and the sugar in a food processor or large mixing bowl. (Choose moist brown sugar if you want the cake to be dark in colour.) Add in the flour and mix well. While you are whisking the egg whites, leave the dried fruit, almonds, candied peel and spices to stand in a warm place and heat the oven to gas mark 3 (325°F, 170°C). Prepare a large cake tin (about 9 inches or 23 cm in diameter) by buttering it well on the inside and cutting a strip of thick brown paper to go around the outside, 1 inch (2.5 cm) or so taller than the tin. Beat into the mixture first the whisked egg whites, then the lightly beaten yolks.

Add in all the other ingredients, finishing with the sherry, and beat well. Pour the mixture into the cake tin, tie the brown paper round the outside firmly and put it straight into the oven. Cook for 2½ hours. This cake can be iced using the recipe on p. 103.

AN IRISH PLUMB CAKE One pound of butter beat to creem, one pound of sugar dryd & sifted, 8 large Eggs or 9 small ones, the yolks beat very well & the Whites wipd up to light froath. One pound of curants, one pound & a quarter of flower both well dryd, a Nuttmeg, a knoggin of brandy, 2 ounces of citron. The Butter must be beat very well for the space of about 20 Minutes. Then Mix in your Ingredients.

IRISH PLUM CAKE

As with plum pudding, the plums in this cake are not plums at all but currants. What makes it Irish is not clear; perhaps it is the brandy. The version below uses half of Mrs Acworth's quantities and produces a good-sized cake for an average household. Using full quantities and baked in a 10 inch (25 cm) square tin, it will produce a great slab of a cake which can be cut into pieces and stored, or used for a great tea-time gathering.

10 oz (280 g, 2 cups) plain wheatmeal flour
4 oz (115 g, ½ cup) each of butter and margarine
8 oz (225 g, 1⅓ cups) dark brown sugar
4 eggs
1 oz (30 g, ¼ cup) mixed candied peel
8 oz (225 g, 1½ cups) mixed sultanas (white raisins) and raisins, or currants
½ nutmeg
3½ fl oz (100 ml, ½ cup) brandy

Sift the flour into a bowl and set it aside. Cream together the butter, margarine and sugar, beat in the egg yolks, having separated the whites into another bowl. Stir in the candied peel, dried fruit, grated nutmeg and brandy, then mix in the flour, spoonful by spoonful. Finally, whisk the egg whites to a stiff froth and beat them well in to the rest of the mixture. Grease an 8 inch (20 cm) diameter cake tin and tie a strip of brown paper firmly round the outside, so that it reaches a little above the rim. Pour in the cake mixture and bake for 1 hour at gas mark 2 (300°F, 150°C). Then reduce the temperature to mark 1 (285°F, 140°C) and bake for a further 2 hours. The brown paper and very low heat help to keep the cake moist.

TO MAKE AN EXCELLENT CAKE Take a pint of the best sweete Creame and a pound of sweete butter, melt ye butter with ye creame a little more than blood warme but first take 4 eggs and one white and beate them with 4 spoonfulls of creame. Then put in mace, cinamon and a little nutmegg and not to much sugar but to your tast, a little salt and a spoonfull of Rose water. So beate it all together very well with ye Creame, then with your hand stir in as much fflower till it is as batter. Then put in 4 pound of currants. Keep it stirring till your oven is fitt for it. Lett the rash heate be over. To much Heate will spoile it. Then butter your molds or Hoops flat and prick it.

AN EXCELLENT FRUIT CAKE

THIS really is an excellent and unusual fruit cake; moist, almost gooey, and flavourful. In this version we give half of the original quantities and rather less than half the quantity of currants.

8 fl oz (225 ml, 1 cup) full cream milk or single (light) cream
4 oz (115 g, $\frac{1}{2}$ cup) each of butter and margarine
2 tablespoons more of milk or cream
2 eggs, plus 1 egg white
1 teaspoon each of ground mace, nutmeg and cinnamon
$\frac{1}{4}$ teaspoon salt
1 tablespoon rose-water
4 oz (115 g, $\frac{5}{8}$ cup) granulated sugar
about 1 lb (450 g, 3 to 3$\frac{1}{2}$ cups) flour
1$\frac{1}{2}$ lbs (675 g) mixed sultanas (white raisins), raisins and currants

Heat the milk slowly and melt the butter and margarine in it. Set it to one side to cool. Meanwhile whisk together the extra milk or cream, eggs, spices, salt, rose-water and sugar. Stir in the mixture of milk or cream and butter and margarine and then sift in the flour, folding it in slowly as the mixture thickens to a smooth batter. You may need a little extra flour, depending on the size of the eggs you have used. Finally, stir in the mixed fruits and put the whole mixture in an 8 inch (20 cm) diameter greased cake tin. (The mixture is too runny for a tin with a removable base.) Cook for approximately 1$\frac{1}{2}$ hours at gas mark 4 (350°F, 180°C).

THE ICEING FOR THE PLUM CAKE To the white of one Egg take one Spoonfull of orange flower water and half a spoonfull of Gum Draggon and mix them together, then take as much double refine sugar sifted fine, as will make it as stiff as Butter. Then beate it in a Bason til its very white. It will be an hour or two a beating. Then spread it on your cake when it is baked, then set it in the Oven til its dry. If the Oven is to hot it will rise it in Blisters.

TO ICE A CAKE Take one pound of fine sugar with the Whites of 5 eggs, 3 or 4 spoonfulls of Oringe flower or rose Water.

PLAIN ICING

IT was common for cakes to be iced and then put in a cool oven to dry, producing a hard, shiny effect. The sugar used was generally 'double refined', the equivalent of modern caster sugar, but the meticulous cook would beat it for a long time in order to produce an even, white effect. The gum dragon used in her first recipe was a thickening agent obtained from shrubs of the Astralagus family, and similar to gum arabic, derived from acacia, which was used for the same culinary purposes. Gum dragon was also used as a sort of starch or stiffener in laundry. It may have been needed in icing when powdered sugar was not readily available, but using modern icing (confectioners') sugar it would seem superfluous. The quantities given in Mrs Acworth's second recipe would ice a large number of cakes and pies. Using one egg white, as below, produces enough to ice a cake 10 inches (25 cm) square.

10 oz (280 g, 2½ cups) icing (confectioners') sugar
white of 1 egg
1 tablespoon rose-water or ½ teaspoon essence of orange flower water

Sift the icing sugar and set it to one side. Beat the egg white until it is very stiff, and stir in the icing sugar. This should make a very stiff paste. Add the rose-water or orange flower water, a drop at a time, until the icing reaches a consistency that can be spread easily but without being too runny. Spread it on the cake and place in a cool oven (gas mark ½, 265°F, 130°C) for about 30 minutes, until the icing is hard.

TO MAKE CAKES Take a pound of butter and a pound of Sugar Searsed fine. Worke ye butter and sugar together with your hands till it looks white and frothy, then put in six eggs with 4 of ye Whites left out. Beate 'em with 2 or 3 spoonfulls of Rose Water and put 'em to ye butter and sugar with a Nutmeg and a little Mace. Then worke 'em in almost an Hour, then strew a pound of Currants Plumped and worke 'em in and almost 2 pound of flower well dryed. Then lay 'em out in Little Cakes in butter'd papers. Ice 'em over with Rose Water and sugar then sett 'em in a pretty Quick Oven. Little bakeing will serve 'em.

LITTLE CAKES

THESE delicious little buns or cakes have a special fragrance which we have learned to associate with eighteenth-century cooking. The aroma of rose-water, nutmeg and mace wafting from the oven is quite irresistible. The sparkle of the cooked icing on top adds to the effect.

4 oz (115 g, $\frac{1}{2}$ cup) each of butter and margarine
8 oz (225 g, just over 1 cup) granulated sugar
1 egg, plus 2 egg yolks
2 tablespoons rose-water
$\frac{1}{2}$ nutmeg
$\frac{1}{2}$ teaspoon ground mace
8 oz (225 g, 2 cups) currants
1 lb (450 g, 3 cups plus 1 tablespoon) flour
2 oz (60 g, $\frac{1}{2}$ cup) icing (confectioners') sugar

Cream together the butter, margarine and sugar. Add the eggs, one tablespoonful of rose-water, grated nutmeg and mace and beat well. Stir in the currants, then the sifted flour, a little at a time. Put the mixture into buttered bun cases. Mix together the remaining tablespoonful of rose-water and the icing sugar and brush the mixture lightly over each bun, using a pastry brush. Bake for about 20 minutes (depending on the size of your bun cases) at gas mark 4 (350°F, 180°C).

TO MAKE GINGER BREAD Take 2 pound and a quarter of Treacle, strain it and put to it a pound and a quarter of butter and worke them with your hand till ye butter is undisarnable. Then put in a quarter of a pound of sugar, an ounce of Coriander seed bruised, an ounce of Caraway seed, an ounce of beaten Ginger, a peice of orange lemon and citron cut small and mix them well together. Then work in your fflower, about a quarter of a peck does it. So make it in little cakes or long roles and bake them on tinn plates or paper buttered. Your oven must be no hotter than for cheesecakes. It is apt to eat to hard at first makeing but it will quickly give againe. I alwaise put in less Ginger and seeds than is in ye receipt for I think it to much, but every one as they please.

GINGERBREAD

IN medieval England, gingerbread used to be made with breadcrumbs and honey, or in a darker version using molasses, it turned into something resembling the Yorkshire delicacy, parkin. The great thing about gingerbread was that it could be fashioned into any shape and would keep for a long time. It became a traditional fairing, each fair boasting its own special varieties. At Charlton Horn fair in Kent, for example, which was supposed to commemorate King John's cuckolding of a miller at Charlton, the gingerbread figures wore horns, in common with the revellers. Gingerbread would often be gilded with gold leaf and decorated in any number of other fanciful ways. This version follows Mrs Acworth's own preference to use less ginger and seeds than the original recipe, and softens the flavour of the treacle by using half golden syrup or honey instead. The result is excellent.

6 oz (3½ fl oz, 100 ml, ⅔ cup) treacle or black molasses
the same quantity of golden (thick corn) syrup or honey
7 oz (200 g, ⅞ cup) butter or soft margarine
12 oz (340 g, 2⅓ cups) plain wheatmeal or white flour
2 teaspoons each ground ginger, crushed coriander, caraway seeds
1 tablespoon chopped mixed candied peel

Blend the treacle, syrup and margarine or butter together in a food processor, then knead in the dry ingredients. Roll out on to a floured board or table, cut into shapes and bake for about half an hour at gas mark 2 (300°F, 150°C). *Alternatively:* Melt the first three ingredients together in a saucepan over a low heat, stir in the dry ingredients then pour the mixture, which will be too liquid to roll, into a deep baking tin about 9 inches (23 cm) square and bake for about 45 minutes at gas mark 2, as above. The gingerbread can be cut into shapes using metal pastry cutters in the pan after it has cooled. Either version can be painted with edible gold food paint when cooked.

TO MAKE MACKROONS Take the whites of eight eggs and beate them very well with a white rod. Take a pound of loafe sugar very firmly beaten a pound and half of blanched almonds wery well beaten with a little rose water. Mix them altogether, put to them a little rose water, so lay it on White Wafers, a spoonfull in a Place. Make them up long Ways, Scrape hard sugar on them and bake them.

MACAROONS

MACAROONS were a favourite form of sweetmeat in eighteenth-century households. They might have been served with tea or a glass of sack or ratafia, and were frequently placed as side or corner dishes in the second course at dinner. They make an excellent accompaniment to any of Mrs Acworth's syllabubs, possets or creams. Almond essence is added in our version because modern, commercially ground almonds do not retain the distinctive flavour which would have been familiar to the eighteenth-century palate. An alternative is to blanch and grind the almonds yourself using a teaspoonful of rose-water as Mrs Acworth did, to prevent them from oiling when they are ground. The resulting texture is more granular than commercially ground almonds and produces more crumbly macaroons.

2 egg whites
6 oz (170 g, 2 cups) ground almonds
4 oz (115 g, $\frac{5}{8}$ cup) granulated sugar
$\frac{1}{8}$ teaspoon almond essence
2 teaspoons rose-water
rice paper
a little demerara (granular brown) sugar, or some flaked almonds,
for decoration

Whisk the egg whites until they are stiff. Stir in the ground almonds, sugar, almond essence and rose-water and mix well. Put the rice paper on to baking trays and place the macaroon mixture on top in teaspoon-sized blobs. Pat each blob into an oval shape and sprinkle a little demerara sugar or place a flake of almond on each one. Bake at gas mark 2 (300°F, 150°C) for 30 minutes, then leave the macaroons to cool before removing them from the trays and trimming the edges of rice paper away with scissors. These quantities, one quarter of Mrs Acworth's, make 20–25 macaroons.

JUMBLES Take 2 pound of fine flower and one pound of Sugar finely beaten, the yolks of eight eggs and a little butter and cream and a few Carraways seeds and a little Rose water. Mix all these and make it into a past and beate it an hour or two with a Rowling pinn, the more you beate it the better. Then take it an Rowle it into long Rowles the bigness of the top of your Little finger and so make them up into what ffashon you please and as fast as you make them up lay them on a pye plate, rubbed over with butter. Then just as you are going to set them in your Oven to bake, take a little Creame and wet them over with a feather. Scrape some hard sugar over them and soo bake them.

JUMBLES

JUMBLES were a great favourite in England and America in the eighteenth and nineteenth centuries. Their name derives from *jumelles* or twins, presumably denoting the double shape, like pretzels, into which they were commonly made. Mrs Acworth had several recipes for them including one with ground almonds. In the twentieth century they have become more typical of American than of British cooking, and are often made with sour cream. The recipe given here produces a rather bland, crunchy cookie suitable for serving with syllabubs and other creams. The flavour of grated orange or lemon zest could be substituted for Mrs Acworth's almost ubiquitous caraway seeds.

10 oz (280 g, 2 cups) plain flour
5 oz (140 g, $\frac{3}{4}$ cup) granulated sugar
2 oz (60 g, $\frac{1}{4}$ cup) butter
2 fl oz (60 ml, $\frac{1}{4}$ cup) single (light) cream
1 tablespoon rose-water
2 egg yolks
1 tablespoon caraway seeds, or grated orange or lemon zest
extra cream and 1 tablespoon demerara (granular brown) sugar
for the topping

Sift the flour into a large mixing bowl or the bowl of a food processor, and stir in the sugar. Melt the butter, cream and rose-water together over a gentle heat, stir in the egg yolks and add immediately to the flour and sugar. Add the caraway seeds or orange and lemon zest and knead all together until a smooth, soft paste is formed. Leave this in the refrigerator for 2–3 hours, then roll it out on a floured board or table. Take strips of the dough and roll them with your fingers into long sausage shapes, then twist them into pretzels. Alternatively, cut the dough with pastry cutters. Brush the jumbles lightly with cream, sprinkle a little demerara sugar over them and bake at gas mark 4 (350°F, 180°C) for about 20 minutes.

CHAPTER SIX

PUDDINGS AND CREAMS

Bath Pudding
Bread and Butter Pudding
Baked Apple Pudding
Stewed Damsons
Carrot Pudding
Almond, Orange and Lemon Tart
Quince Pie
Whipped Syllabub
Blancmange
Sack Posset
Trifle
Puff Pastry
Cheesecake
Orange and Almond Cheesecake
A Fancy
Snow Cream

Blancmange; Orange and Almond Cheesecake

M RS Acworth had even more recipes for puddings and creams than for cakes and pastries. She lived, after all, in the golden age of English puddings. Since the invention of the pudding cloth in the seventeenth century, puddings had developed as a distinctive part of English cooking. Originally they had depended on the availability of animal guts to contain the mixture of grains or flour, meat and sweeteners, which would then be sewn up tight inside their tough casing, and boiled in a cauldron with the mutton or the fowl, until the ingredients had blended together. Almond hog's pudding, for example, was still a favourite in the eighteenth century, and Mrs Acworth had a recipe for it. It was a confection of ground almonds and cream cooked in skin like a sausage, an eagerly awaited treat because it depended on the killing of a pig. The simple notion of flouring a cloth and tying up the pudding inside it was a revolution. By the end of the seventeenth century, at least one French traveller was singing the praises of pudding: 'Ah, what an excellent thing is an English pudding! To come in pudding-time, is as much as to say, to come in the most lucky moment in the world.'

Pudding was not a very precise term. There were, and there still are, savoury puddings as well as sweet ones and puddings that combined sweet and savoury ingredients. There were very plain puddings, like Yorkshire pudding which was cooked in the dripping pan beneath the meat and intended to provide the ballast in the meal. There were puddings of almost infinite complexity, designed for great feasts. Puddings could also be cooked as tarts, inside or on top of pastry casings; they could be baked in the oven as well as in the cauldron. And they served the poorest cook as well as the most extravagant.

Mrs Acworth had recipes for many varieties of pudding, both boiled and baked. Some would have been served as dinner-party fare. Others were intended for more modest occasions, like the Bread and Butter Pudding for fasting days. The basic ingredient to supply the bulk varied greatly. Breadcrumbs and suet were both common, oatmeal sometimes used. Ground rice was used in several recipes, like the Bath Pudding. Ground almonds, eggs, milk and cream were frequently included. Others, like the Fancy and the Bread and Butter Pudding, and a quaking pudding and a white pot which we have not included, were thickened with bread. In some cases she recommended a sauce of melted butter, sack and sugar, or rose-water and sugar. Other puddings stood by themselves. Tarts and pies could also be puddings. The Almond, Orange and Lemon Tart and the Quince Pie show Mrs Acworth using some of her favourite fruits.

Cheesecakes were another favourite in the Acworth household. Curd cheese was a staple of the English housewife's kitchen, and Mrs Acworth was no exception. She had a recipe for making her own curds, and several for cheesecakes. Curd cheese was so indispensable that when fresh milk was scarce (as it was in the spring, season for newborn calves) it was necessary to improvise from other ingredients. Mrs Acworth made 'fresh cheese and cream in Lent' from ground almonds. She also used ground rice and ground almonds without any cheese at all to make what she still called cheesecakes. Cooked in the form of little tarts, her cheesecakes might have been offered as a side dish or arranged among the sweetmeats at dinner, or offered to her guests at afternoon tea. Like most of Mrs Acworth's cake and pastry recipes, they are delicious and have a marked tendency to disappear.

Then there were jellies and creams. Blancmange, which was both jelly and cream, was one of the oldest recipes. It was what its name implied, simply a 'white eat'. Medieval recipes for blancmange were originally a sort of pottage including chicken, but by the mid-eighteenth century, like so many other old recipes which formerly mixed meat with sweet ingredients, it had become simply a sweet dish. Made with isinglass or hartshorn (for which gelatine substitutes well), it could be poured into little cups or one large copper jelly mould and turned out in decorative shapes. Mrs Acworth's blancmange is an ancestor of countless upstanding, only slightly wobbly, centrepieces on the dinner tables and nursery tea tables of England. By the time it had descended to the indefinite 'shape' of the 1930s and 1940s it was in poor repute. Aunt Fenny's shapes, a little piece of disappearing Anglo-India in Paul Scott's *A Division of the Spoils*, 'were white and looked tasteless, but there was a bowl of jam to liven them up'. Mrs Acworth, with her thickening of ground almonds rather than the flour or cornflour of later versions, and her flavouring of laurel leaves, did better.

Other jellies were made with calves' feet, like flummery, or with fruit and sugar, like the Pippin Jelly on p. 138, which was essentially a preserve. Alongside the blancmange, a range of delicate custards and creams adorned her table. Syllabub, for which she had several recipes, and Sack Posset, which resembled syllabub in flavour but used eggs as well as cream, were both descended from sweet drinks made with cream and wine but had turned into firmer dishes by her day. They would have been served in little individual dishes or glasses and eaten with a spoon.

In recipes using cooked fruit, Mrs Acworth took care to preserve the flavour of the fruit by keeping it out of contact with water as far as possible. Apples would be roasted or coddled in their skins and their flesh then scraped out, rather than stewed using a little water. Other fruits were cooked in skillets standing in boiling water. In her recipe for stewed damsons she places them between two dishes to cook. Fruit had always been an important part of the English diet. In Mrs Acworth's cooking it played a central part. By her day, the old view that raw fruit was bad for the health had virtually disappeared. Well-to-do families would vie with each other for the splendour of the pyramids of fruit that graced their desserts, culled perhaps from their own glass-houses or even orangeries. (Witness the feast laid on by the lovelorn Mr Darcy for Elizabeth Bennet in *Pride and Prejudice*, a few decades later.) Nevertheless there was still almost endless scope for invention with cooked fruit as well. The Acworth family seem to have enjoyed access to large supplies of oranges and lemons, apricots, peaches, nectarines, quinces, gooseberries, raspberries, currants, almonds and other nuts, and different varieties of apples and plums. Of the fruits which were in common use then, only pears are not mentioned.

A fruit recipe of some antiquity was Snow Cream. A light concoction of apples, egg whites and sugar is well known in modern English cooking as apple snow. Snow Cream is as delicate, and even prettier to behold. Anne Wilson describes in *Food and Drink in Britain* how the Elizabethans would produce its forerunner, 'a dishful of snow', as the centrepiece for a banquet. Whites of egg 'were beaten with thick cream, rose-water and sugar until the froth rose, and the latter was gathered in a colander, and then built up over an apple and "a thick bush of rosemary" on a platter. In some versions the snow was gilded as a final touch.' Today, the recipe is simplicity itself. But Mrs Acworth's instructions to beat the ingredients together 'for two or three hours' and then to 'lay the Froth lightly in a China Dish' show the hard labour as well as artistry that were still involved in whisking egg whites and cream in the mid-eighteenth century, and amply explain why Snow Cream deserved to be given a triumphal place among the desserts.

A RECEIPT FOR AN EXCELLENT BATH PUDDING Two ounces of ground Rice, a pint of Milk, 3 Eggs but 2 whites; mix the Rice in a little cold Milk, boil the rest, stir it all together & boil it up. When almost cold, put in the Eggs, some grated Lemon peel, sweeten with powder sugar & boil it in a Bason 3 qrs of an hour.

BATH PUDDING

THIS simple recipe, beautifully written out in a fair hand that does not appear elsewhere among Mrs Acworth's papers, was tucked loose inside her book. It is a classic English pudding recipe, delicately flavoured and good by itself, but even better served with a topping of melted raspberry or apricot jam. It was probably called Bath pudding because it was boiled in a bath of water, rather than after the town. On the other hand, a similar recipe using flour instead of ground rice appears in Florence White's *Good Things in England* as Buxton Pudding.

2 oz (60 g, $\frac{1}{3}$ cup) ground rice
16 fl oz (450 ml, 2 cups) milk
zest of $\frac{1}{2}$ a lemon
3 eggs, leaving out 1 white
2 oz (60 g, scant $\frac{1}{3}$ cup) granulated sugar

Mix the ground rice in a pudding basin with enough of the milk to make a smooth paste. Bring the rest of the milk to the boil very slowly with a shaving of lemon peel in it. When it boils, pour it over the ground rice paste, stir well and pour the mixture back into the saucepan, stirring constantly until it returns to the boil. Leave it to cool for about 10 minutes, until it is no more than hand-hot. Whisk the grated lemon, eggs and sugar together lightly and pour the cooled mixture over them. Remove the shaving of lemon peel and pour the whole mixture into a lightly greased pudding basin, soufflé dish or ovenproof jelly mould of 1$\frac{1}{2}$ pints (840 ml, scant 2 US pints) capacity or more. Cover it with greaseproof (waxed) paper and stand in a saucepan of hot water. Bring the water to the boil then leave it to simmer, just bubbling, for about 1$\frac{1}{2}$ hours. Turn the pudding on to a dish and serve it hot with jam or stewed fruit.

To make a bread and butter pudding for fasting days Take a two penny Lofe and [one] pound of fresh Butter. Spread it in thin slices as to eat. Cut them of as you spread them and stone half a pound of Resons and wash a pound of Currans. Then putt puff past at the bottom of a Dish & lay a row of bread & Butter & strew a handfull of Currants & a few resons and some Little bits of Butter, and do so until your dish is full. Then boyle 3 pints of Creeme & thicken it when Cold with the Yolks of ten Eggs, a Grated Nutmeg. a little sack, near half a pound of Shugger, some Orange flower water, and poor this in just as the Puding is going into the Oven.

BREAD AND BUTTER PUDDING

THIS recipe tells us a little about Margaretta Acworth's way of life, as well as her kitchen. It is one of several recommended for fasting days, so she was probably a good observer of the rules of the Anglican Church of her day, and would have fasted during Lent and on other dates in the year. On the other hand, this bread and butter pudding is more of a feast than a fast in modern terms. It is a positive celebration of butter, which was used lavishly in Georgian cookery but rarely more so than here. The large quantity of cream, eggs, butter and bread suggests that the dish would have been consumed by the whole household (perhaps instead of a main meal). Note how the raisins had to be stoned, a reminder of the hard work involved in cooking even the most straightforward dishes.

10 slices of white bread weighing 10 oz (280 g) altogether
5 oz (140 g, $\frac{1}{2}$ cup plus 1 tablespoon) butter
3 oz (85 g, $\frac{2}{3}$ cup) raisins
6 oz (170 g, $1\frac{1}{3}$ cups) currants
16 fl oz (450 ml, 2 cups or 1 US pint) single (light) cream
3 egg yolks
$\frac{1}{2}$ nutmeg
2 fl oz (60 ml, $\frac{1}{4}$ cup) dry sherry
2 oz (60 g, scant $\frac{1}{3}$ cup) granulated sugar
$\frac{1}{4}$ teaspoon essence of orange flower water

Spread the slices of bread thickly with the softened butter, reserving a little to strew into the pudding. Grease the sides of a pie or soufflé dish with butter and lay the slices of bread and butter in it buttered side upwards, alternating each layer with a sprinkling of raisins and currants and a few extra little dollops of butter. Bring the cream to the boil and leave it to one side to cool. Whisk together the egg yolks, grated nutmeg, sherry, sugar and orange flower water, and then pour the cream over them, stirring thoroughly. Pour this mixture over the bread and butter and put the pudding immediately into a moderate oven (gas mark 4, 350°F, 180°C) to cook for about 40 minutes. It should emerge golden-crusted, aromatic and irresistible.

TO MAKE A BAKE APPLE PUDDING Take 7 fair Coddlings and Coddle em, then take 1/2 a pd. of melted Butter; 1/2 a pd. of Sugar; ye yolks of 6 Eggs; 1/2 a nutmeg; and the peel of 1/2 a Lemon grated. Mixt it all together and put puff past at the bottom.

BAKED APPLE PUDDING

THE egg yolks in this recipe make it rise prodigiously, producing a sort of soufflé. Unlike most soufflés, however, this pudding is just as good cold as hot.

4 large cooking apples
3 egg yolks
4 oz (115 g, ⅝ cup) granulated sugar
4 oz (115 g, ½ cup) butter
grated zest of ½ lemon
½ nutmeg
puff (see p. 125) or shortcrust pastry made with 8 oz (225 g,
1⅔ cups) flour (optional, see below)

Cover the apples with cold water in a large pan and bring them to the boil. Leave them to simmer for about 10 minutes, until they are tender. Cut them into quarters and scrape all the flesh away from the skin, discarding only the pips and strings at the core, and the thin, outermost skin. Mash the apple flesh in a bowl or blend it in a food processor, stir in the egg yolks, sugar and melted butter and then grate in the lemon zest and nutmeg and mix well. Line a deep flan dish (at least 7 inches, 18 cm diameter and 2 inches, 5 cm deep) with shortcrust or puff pastry, pour in the apple mixture and bake at gas mark 4 (350°F, 180°C) for 1 hour. *Alternatively*, omit the pastry altogether and cook the pudding in a soufflé dish, as above.

TO STEW DAMSONS AND PLUMS Take Damsons and stew them beetweene 2 dishes with Water Sugar and a few Cloves bruised and the Rind of an Orrange or Lemon cut into thin peeces. Let them stew together. Put in some Rose Water and soo serve them in.

STEWED DAMSONS

MORE than 160 varieties of plum were known in Britain by the seventeenth century. The damson was one of the smallest, dark in colour and especially suitable for cooking because of its tart, strong flavour. Its name is short for Damascene, that is, the plum from Damascus.

1 lb (450 g) damsons (or tart plums)
4 fl oz (115 ml, ½ cup) water
1 oz (30 g, 2 tablespoons) sugar
rind of 1 orange
6 cloves
1 tablespoon rose-water

Put the damsons together with the water, sugar, thinly pared orange rind and cloves in a saucepan and bring them to the boil, lowering the heat immediately to let them stew gently until they are tender. Remove them from the heat before stirring in the rose-water. Serve either hot or cold.

*T*O *MAKE A CARRETT PUDDING* *Greate two penny loaves of bread and an equall Quantity of carretts 1 Nutmeg ¹/₂ a pound of melted butter 4 or 5 spoonfulls of Rose Water and a little salt. Mingle these well together put all into a pann that is buttered lett it bake 2 hours then turn it out. The properest sauce is Roase water and Sugar.*

CARROT PUDDING

T HIS pudding has a good, light texture. It is as good cold as hot, and can be served cold at tea time or with coffee, or when hot, as a dessert at dinner.

6 oz (170 g, 3 cups) breadcrumbs
6 oz (170 g, 2 cups) grated carrots
4 oz (115 g, $\frac{5}{8}$ cups) granulated sugar
about $\frac{1}{2}$ nutmeg, grated
16 fl oz (450 ml, 2 cups or 1 US pint) milk or milk and
cream mixed
2 oz (60 g, $\frac{1}{4}$ cup) butter (optional)
3 large eggs, leaving out 1 white
1 tablespoon rose-water

Grate the bread and carrot together into the food processor or a large bowl. Stir in the sugar and nutmeg. Warm the milk to blood heat, melting the butter in it if you wish; pour it over the lightly beaten eggs, stirring gently, add rose-water and then pour this mixture over the dry ingredients in the bowl. Mix well and spoon the finished mixture into a medium-sized cake tin: it looks particularly good cooked in a ring-shaped tin, 9 inches (23 cm) in diameter. Cook for 2 hours at gas mark 3 (325°F, 170°C). Test with a toothpick to check that it is firm, and turn out on to a warmed plate. Serve immediately, with a little sugar melted in some rose-water, or with cream.

ALMOND PUDDING Boyl one quart of cream and when cold putt to it the whites of 7 eggs beat to a froath blanch 5 ounces of sweet Almonds beat them fine. Add a little orange flower water then mix them with the cream and eggs. Sweeten it with fine sugar. Lay puff paste in ye dish then lay on the top thin slices of orange, lemon and citron. It must be baked in a cool oven slowly heated. When the crust is baked it is enough.

ALMOND, ORANGE AND LEMON TART

THIS is what we would call a tart or flan, rather than a pudding. It is one of Mrs Acworth's most delectable sweet recipes, with a light texture which complements well the delicate flavours of the ingredients. The slices of orange and lemon on the top look very pretty. The following recipe using half of her quantities makes more than enough for six. The dish needs to be a little deeper than the average flan dish if possible, in order to get just the right texture. The tart may be served hot or cold.

16 fl oz (450 ml, 2 cups or 1 US pint) whipping cream
3 oz (85 g, $\frac{1}{2}$ cup) granulated sugar
3 oz (85 g, 1 cup) ground almonds
$\frac{1}{4}$ teaspoon almond essence
$\frac{1}{4}$ teaspoon essence of orange flower water
1 tablespoon mixed candied peel (optional)
4 small or 3 large egg whites
1 large or 2 small lemons
1 large or 2 small oranges
puff (see p. 125) or shortcrust pastry made with 6 oz (170 g,
$1\frac{1}{4}$ cups) flour

Stand the cream over a moderate heat with a slice of lemon peel in it and bring slowly to the boil. Set it to cool. Mix the sugar, ground almonds and flavourings together with some candied peel if you like it. Whisk the egg whites to a light froth and fold them in, with the cream (from which you have removed the lemon peel). Line a 9 inch (23 cm) diameter flan dish with puff or shortcrust pastry. (Mrs Acworth usually specifies puff pastry for her tart or flan type puddings, but the effort of making puff pastry seems rather wasted when shortcrust is just as good.) Pour the filling into the pastry-lined dish and gently lay thin slices of orange and lemon all over the surface. Sprinkle a little extra sugar on top and bake at gas mark 3 (325°F, 170°C) for about an hour.

To BAKE A WARDEN OF QUINCES Pare well and boyle them. Cutt the sharp end flat. Boyle in White wine & shugger till the surrup grew thick, then lay them out to coole and make a Coffin for them of tough thick past. Then lay them in. Stick whole Cloves [and] Cinamon in them. Putt on shugger and some of the surrup that they where boyled in. Close the pye and bake it moderately.

QUINCE PIE

THIS recipe is a delicious curiosity. The name warden was normally given to a sort of pear used for cooking in pies and tarts, rather than to the pie itself, but clearly Mrs Acworth meant a pie made with quinces. She also departs from the more common recipes of her day in flavouring the quinces with cloves rather than ginger, and cooking them whole inside the pie rather than in a pulp or paste. The result is excellent: the quinces make a clear red syrup which turns to jelly as it cools, toning with the lighter amber colour of the fruit itself. The flavours of wine, sugar, cloves and cinnamon combine to remove the tartness of the quinces and bring out their distinctive, rather fragrant taste.

6 quinces weighing about 1½ lbs (675 g) altogether
5 oz (140 g, ¾ cup) granulated sugar
2 fl oz (60 ml, ¼ cup) white wine
1 stick of cinnamon
6 cloves
about 1 lb (450 g) puff pastry (p. 125)

Peel and core the quinces. Place them in a saucepan with just enough cold water to cover them, bring to the boil and then simmer them for about 10 minutes, until they are beginning to soften, but still firm. Make a syrup by bringing the sugar and white wine to the boil, place the quinces gently in the syrup and leave to boil over a moderate heat for about 5 minutes. Meanwhile, line a lightly greased pie dish with puff pastry. Lift the quinces out of the syrup and place them in the pie, taking care to keep them whole. Break the cinnamon into small pieces and place a little of it inside each quince. Stick 1 clove into each quince. Pour the syrup over them while it is still warm and before it turns to jelly. Cover the pie with more puff pastry and cook at gas mark 4 (350°F, 180°C) for half an hour.

To MAKE WHIP SULLYBUBS Take a pint of Cream, put to that half a pint of sack or mountain, half a nutmeg grated, some Lemon peel grated, two or three lemons, sugar as you like. Beet these together to a sullibub then put them in your glasses. You may if you will Boyl your cream first.

WHIPPED SYLLABUB

LIKE gingerbread, syllabub is one of those dishes that have attracted learned treatises. From the early versions of the sixteenth century or even earlier, which were drinks of wine topped with frothing cream, the dish developed to a less liquid cream, suitable for serving with dessert and for eating with a spoon from glasses. Mrs Acworth's various syllabub recipes, including this one, will be familiar to the modern English cook.

16 fl oz (450 ml, 2 cups) double (heavy) cream (whipping cream is too thin)
$\frac{1}{2}$ nutmeg
1 large or 2 small lemons
8 fl oz (225 ml, 1 cup) dry sherry
about 3 oz (85 g, $\frac{1}{2}$ cup) caster sugar

Whip the cream until it is firm but soft. Grate in the nutmeg and the zest of half a large lemon or one small one. Pour in about half of the juice of the lemon(s), half the sherry, add the sugar, and whip the mixture again until it returns to the soft consistency you first reached. Add in the remaining liquid and extra sugar if you wish, then whip it again. When it again reaches a suitably firm consistency, put it into glasses or little ramekin dishes, and keep it in the refrigerator. The flavour improves with keeping for two days or more. Serve with Macaroons or Jumbles (see pp. 106–7). These quantities make enough for at least twelve servings.

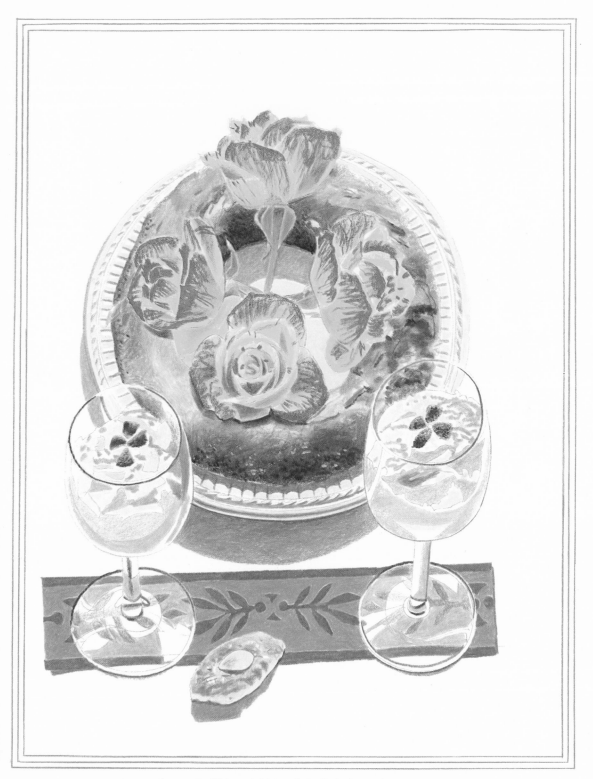

Carrot Pudding; Whipped Syllabubs with Macaroon

TO MAKE BLAMANGG Take a Pint of Milk, half a pint of Cream, 2 ounces of sweet almonds, 6 laurel leaves, a little mace and nutmegg, half an ounce of iseinglass finely shav'd, and sweeten it to your Tast. Boyl it till it Comes to a thick Cream, then strain it of into cups, and let it stand all night, and then it is ready to Turn out of the Cups for use.

BLANCMANGE

THIS is one of several blancmange recipes in Mrs Acworth's book, unusual because it includes laurel leaves. These were not an outlandish ingredient in eighteenth-century cooking. They were valued for their bitter almond flavour, but they were also toxic, and had to be removed before the dish was served. Mrs Acworth clearly realized this, since her blancmange was strained into cups. She may even have meant bay rather than laurel leaves, for the two were sometimes confused. We have used bay leaves in our version, together with enough almond essence to give a pronounced almond flavour, as the laurel leaves would have done. It is well worth trying.

16 fl oz (450 ml, 2 cups) milk
8 fl oz (225 ml, 1 cup) single (light) cream
6 bay leaves (optional)
$\frac{1}{4}$ teaspoon almond essence
$\frac{1}{4}$ teaspoon essence of orange flower water
$\frac{1}{2}$ nutmeg
1$\frac{1}{2}$ sachets (i.e. $\frac{1}{2}$ oz, 15 g, 1 tablespoon) powdered gelatine
2 oz (60 g, scant $\frac{1}{3}$ cup) caster or granulated sugar
2 oz (60 g, $\frac{3}{4}$ cup) ground almonds

Put the milk and cream together in a saucepan, add the bay leaves, almond essence, essence of orange flower water and grated nutmeg and leave them to stand for at least half an hour. Melt enough powdered gelatine, according to the instructions on the packet, for 24 fl oz (675 ml, 3 cups or 1$\frac{1}{2}$ US pints) in a little of the milk over a very low heat. It will appear curdled but this does not matter. Bring the rest of the milk, with its flavourings, very slowly to the boil. Turn off the heat and pour in the gelatine, beating with a wire whisk. Pour all this through a sieve on to the ground almonds and sugar, still beating, until it is quite smooth and the sugar has dissolved. Pour into a jelly mould or individual moulds and put in the refrigerator to set.

To MAKE A SACK POSSET Take a pint or a pint and ¹/₂ of Milke, boyle it with a peece of nutmeg. Take 8 or 9 eggs, beate them very well and Straine them into your Bason. Put to them ¹/₂ a pint of sack and as much sugar as you think fit. Set it over a Chaffin dish of Coales constantly stirring till it be ready to boyle. Take out your nutmeg and pour your Milke High. Stire your eggs all the While your Milke goos in, take it of the coales, cover it and lett it stand on the stones ¹/₂ an Hour before you Eate it.

SACK POSSET

I n their liquid form, possets usually consisted of milk or cream curdled with ale or wine, but these had declined in favour by the mid-eighteenth century. Eating possets (as opposed to possets for drinking) often had bread, Naples biscuits or ground almonds mixed in to thicken them. This recipe, one of the most straightforward of all, makes a deliciously flavoured custard.

16 fl oz (450 ml, 2 cups or 1 US pint) milk
½ nutmeg
8 medium-sized eggs
3 oz (85 g, ½ cup) granulated sugar
8 fl oz (225 ml, 1 cup) medium-dry or sweet sherry

Put the piece of nutmeg in the milk in a saucepan and bring to the boil. Leave it to one side, covered and over a very low heat, to keep warm. Whisk the eggs in a pudding basin, soufflé dish or similar heatproof dish, until they froth. Stir in the sugar and sherry. Stand the dish containing this mixture in a shallow pan of boiling water over a moderate heat and stir gently for about 5 to 10 minutes, until it thickens. If it develops little lumps, whisk it briskly with a wire whisk. When this has reached the consistency of very thick custard and is quite hot, remove the nutmeg from the milk and pour it into the custard mixture from as high as you can manage, stirring all the time with the wire whisk. Remove the posset from the heat and leave it to cool down. It can be eaten after half an hour, or kept in the refrigerator until the next day. It is especially good served with Macaroons or Almond Jumbles (see pp. 106–7).

TO MAKE A TRIFLE Take Savoy biscakes and lay them in a China Dish. Cover the Bottom [and] wet them through with white wine. Boyl a thick Custard and pour it over them, then whip up a sullibub and put it on the Custard. It must be made overnight. You may make it what sise you will.

TRIFLE

THE same friend who sent the recipe for a Fancy also supplied this one for trifle. We have been unable to discover a difference between the 'Savoy biscakes' she used in her trifle and the 'Naples biskits' in the Fancy. Both were a sort of sponge finger biscuit. Did the two kingdoms of Italy vie with each other for the popularity of their biscuits in the English market?

4 oz (115 g) sponge biscuits
about 10 fl oz (280 g, 1¼ cups) dry white wine
16 fl oz (450 ml, 2 cups or 1 US pint) milk
4 eggs plus 1 extra yolk
about 4 oz (115 g, ⅝ cup) caster or granulated sugar
½ nutmeg
zest and juice of ½ lemon

Lay the biscuits in the bottom of a serving dish and pour over them half of the wine. Make a classic rich boiled custard, i.e. heat the milk to blood heat (98.6°F, 37°C), beat the eggs well with 2 oz (60 g, scant ⅓ cup) sugar and a little grated nutmeg, pour the warm milk over the eggs and return the mixture to the saucepan, stirring constantly over a low heat until it begins to thicken. Allow the custard to become quite cold before pouring it over the biscuits in the dish, and leave it for some hours, preferably overnight, in the refrigerator to set. Meanwhile, make a syllabub using the cream, lemon, wine and remaining sugar and nutmeg according to the recipe on p. 120. Leave that too in the refrigerator overnight, and spoon it evenly over the custard when you are ready to serve the trifle.

To make puff past Take 3 pound of flour, put to it 3 egs. Save out 2 youlks then make it into past with Cold water, & role in a pound of butter att 9 or 10 times, and a small coat of flower before every roleing.

PUFF PASTRY

Puff pastry was what Mrs Acworth normally used for tarts and for those puddings that required pastry. Cheesecakes and mince pies would also have been made with puff pastry. These days, the method is too time-consuming for a busy cook on her own to use often. But this standard recipe makes a pleasing change from shortcrust for a special occasion.

10 oz (280 g, 2 cups) flour, preferably strong white bread flour
1 egg white
about 4 fl oz (115 g, ½ cup) cold water
3 oz (85 g, ⅜ cup) butter or margarine

Sift the flour and stir in the mixed egg white and water. Knead to a smooth dough, using more water if necessary. Roll out the dough to a rectangle about 15 inches (38 cm) long and 5 inches (12.5 cm) wide, and mark it in three equal lengths by scoring it gently with a knife. Cut the butter or margarine into small dice and divide these into five equal portions. (Use one fifth for each repeat of the rolling process.) Then dot half of one fifth of the butter over the central section of the pastry, fold over one end, dot the remaining part of the one fifth portion of butter on top of this, and cover it over with the other end of the rectangle. Turn the thick pad of pastry through 90 degrees and roll it out as thin as you can into a rectangle approximately the same size as before. Carry out this procedure 5 times altogether, using as much flour as you need on the board and rolling pin to stop the pastry from sticking to them. Leave the completed pastry in the refrigerator for about 30 minutes before rolling it out for use.

To make cheese cakes Take your Curd & hang it up in a Straner to Lett the whey run from it. Then to 2 quarts of it put one pound of Butter. Beat the Curd & Butter well together then putt to it 8 yolks of Egs and 4 whites, a Glass of Sack, & Orange flower water, a pound & half of Currans, a hand full or two of greated bread. Mix alltogether and Season it with Cinamon, Nutmeg & Shugger.

___

CHEESECAKE

THIS recipe, which does use real cheese, can be made into one large cheesecake and served in slices, or used to make delicious little individual tarts. Cheesecakes like these were served not only in private houses but on great public occasions as well. Florence White's *Good Things in England* includes a recipe from Melton Mowbray in Leicestershire, where cheesecakes were traditionally offered at Whitsuntide.

1 lb (450 g, 2 cups) soft curd or cottage cheese
2 eggs
4 oz (115 g, $\frac{1}{2}$ cup) butter
4 fl oz (115 ml, $\frac{1}{2}$ cup) sherry
$\frac{1}{2}$ teaspoon essence of orange flower water
1 teaspoon each of ground cinnamon and grated nutmeg
2 oz (60 g, $1\frac{1}{4}$ cups) fine white breadcrumbs
3 oz (85 g, $\frac{1}{2}$ cup) granulated or caster sugar
3 oz (85 g, $\frac{3}{4}$ cup) currants
shortcrust pastry or puff pastry (see p. 125) made with 8 oz
(225 g, $1\frac{2}{3}$ cups) flour

Mix together the cheese, eggs, melted butter, sherry, flavourings, breadcrumbs and sugar, beating well in a large bowl or blending them in a food processor. Stir in the currants. Make a shortcrust or puff pastry sufficient to line an 8 inch (20 cm) diameter cake tin or 24 individual tart cases. Pour the cheesecake mixture right up to the top of the pastry, and cook at gas mark 4 (350°F, 180°C) for 1 hour in the case of a single cake, or 30 minutes if you are making tarts. The mixture rises only very slightly during cooking and then cools to a firm, close-grained texture, so it is as well to make the cheesecakes deep.

ORANGE CHEESECAKES Blanch half a pound of almonds beaten very fine with 2 spoonfulls of oring flower water, half a pound of sugar finely sifted, 3 quarters of a pound of Butter melted. Putt it to the rest when almost cold. 8 Eggs leaveing out 4 whites. Boyle the peal of a Sevil orange till the bitterness is almost out then beat it fine & mix it with the rest and putt it into a very light crust. NB It is very good without the Orange.

ORANGE AND ALMOND CHEESECAKE

LIKE marmalade, cheese seems to have been a word that denoted texture rather than the precise ingredient in Mrs Acworth's recipes. This tart has no cheese, but sets to a texture just like cheesecake. It is one of her most delicious sweet recipes and has become a great standby in our repertoire. A mixture of half and half butter and margarine rather than all butter gives a lighter texture but preserves the flavour of butter in the end result. If you are using commercially ground almonds, here as in the other recipes using almonds, add a dash of almond essence but omit the orange flower water if you wish. The original purpose of this was to prevent the almonds from oiling as they were ground.

3 oz (85 g, $\frac{3}{8}$ cup) each of butter and margarine
3 large or 4 small eggs, leaving out 2 whites
grated zest and juice of 1 small orange
4 oz (115 g, $\frac{5}{8}$ cup) granulated sugar
$\frac{1}{2}$ teaspoon essence of orange flower water (optional)
$\frac{1}{4}$ teaspoon almond essence
4 oz (115 g, 1 cup) ground almonds
shortcrust pastry made with 8 oz (225 g, 1$\frac{2}{3}$ cups) flour
cream, to serve (optional)

Cream together the butter and margarine, add in the other filling ingredients and mix well. Line a deep 9 inch (23 cm) diameter flan dish with shortcrust pastry, pour in the filling and bake for about 30 minutes at gas mark 4 (350°F, 180°C). This will serve six to eight people. It is good eaten warm or cold, and a little thin cream goes well with it.

To MAKE A FANCY Take a quart of Cream and Boyl it. Then take half a pound of Naple Biskits sliced. Pour the Cream hot over them and Cover it. Put to it half a pound of Butter and sugar to your tast. When it is a little cold take 14 eggs, leave out 7 whites, beet them well and strain them. Put them to the cream with a small nutmegg grated and almost a pint of Spinage juice, a little Tanzy Juice, Butter your dish. Half an hour will bake it.

A FANCY

So light a name belies the robust qualities of this pudding, rich with cream and eggs, but the unusual flavour and texture are delicious enough to tickle most people's fancy, and well deserve the title. Mrs Acworth's Fancy (a recipe supplied by a friend) was very similar to the dish called tansy, originally a sort of omelette made with the chopped leaves of the bitter herb tansy. By the early eighteenth century, with the rise of sweet puddings, tansy was turning into a sweet dish made with sugar, cream and breadcrumbs and steamed in a pudding cloth. Its distinctive green tint was supplied by spinach juice and fewer tansy leaves were used. Since tansy is virtually unobtainable now, at least in shops, we have omitted it from our version of this Fancy.

4 oz (115 g) sponge biscuits
16 fl oz (450 ml, 2 cups or 1 US pint) double (heavy) cream
the same quantity of spinach juice, strained from about 1 lb
(450 g) of spinach cooked without salt
2 oz (60 g, $\frac{1}{4}$ cup) butter
3 eggs, plus 4 egg yolks
4 oz (115 g, $\frac{5}{8}$ cup) sugar
$\frac{1}{2}$ nutmeg

Break the biscuits into small pieces and put them in a buttered pie dish. Cut the butter into small pieces into the cream, add the spinach juice and bring it all to the boil. Allow it to cool until it is barely tepid. Meanwhile whisk the eggs and mix in the sugar and grated nutmeg. Pour the cream and butter and spinach juice over the egg mixture, stir well and then pour it all over the broken biscuits. Bake at gas mark 4 (350°F, 180°C) for about 30 minutes. It is good served hot or cold, though the crust formed by the biscuits when they rise to the top in baking is particularly attractive while it is still sizzling hot.

SNOW CREAM A Quarter of a pound of Roasted Apple, a Quarter of a pound of the finest sugar beaten; the juice of two Lemons, and the Whites of Six Eggs. Beat these together for two or three hours. Lay the Froth lightly in a China Dish. Then put some Lemon peal grated, some Orange Flower water & a little very fine sugar, into half a Pint of thick Cream, let it stand sometime, Strain it, and pour it very gently round the Dish. This Snow Cream must not be made many hours before you use it.

SNOW CREAM

THIS pretty delicacy should be dished up an hour or more before you intend to serve it. The meringue appears to float on the cream and as the dish is left to stand, the cream runs in rivulets into the meringue and forms a light crust in places.

> 1 large or 2 small cooking apples such as Bramleys (about $\frac{1}{2}$ lb or
> 225 g in uncooked weight will produce about $\frac{1}{4}$ lb, 115 g or $\frac{1}{2}$ cup,
> when cooked)
> 1 large or 2 small lemons
> whites of 4 eggs
> 4 oz (115 g, $\frac{5}{8}$ cup) caster sugar
> 4 oz (115 ml, $\frac{1}{2}$ cup) double (heavy) cream
> $\frac{1}{2}$ teaspoon essence of orange flower water

Put the apples whole into a saucepan and cover them with cold water. Bring them to the boil, then simmer gently until they are tender. When they have cooled, cut them into quarters and scrape the flesh away from the skin and cores. Measure 4 oz (115 g, $\frac{1}{2}$ cup) of the cooked apple into a mixing bowl or food processor. Add the juice of the lemon(s), the egg whites and most of the sugar, reserving a tablespoonful of it to add to the cream. Whip all these ingredients together vigorously, either with an electric or manual rotary whisk or using the food processor, for about 5 minutes, until they form a stiff froth which holds its shape like meringue. Pour the cream into a separate bowl and mix in the orange flower water, grated lemon zest and remaining sugar. Leave it to stand in the refrigerator for an hour or more, then spoon the meringue mixture on to a serving dish with a good brim or raised edge. Gently pour the cream around it. Serve it with Macaroons.

CHAPTER SEVEN

JELLIES, MARMALADES AND PRESERVES

Apple and Quince Jelly
Apricot Jam
Cherry Preserve
Red Currant Jelly
Grape Jam
Pippin Jelly with Orange
Plum Jelly
Raspberry Jam
Quince Marmalade

Pippin Jelly with Orange; Cherry Preserve; Apricot Jam

ELLIES, marmalades and preserves are highlights of the British and American breakfast. But this was not always so. In Mrs Acworth's day these delicacies of soft fruit, whether bought from a professional confectioner or home-made by ladies and their maids, were consumed with dinner as desserts. The classic English marmalade, a word derived from the Portuguese quince, or *marmelo*, was typically put into moulds or sold in bricks and carved into slices as a sweetmeat. Traditionally, marmalade was synonymous with quince, but in Mrs Acworth's vocabulary it was extended to include other fruits as well. Her manuscript is well stocked with recipes for cherry, apricot, and red and white quince marmalade, and also contains various preserves and jellies made from grapes, nectarines, oranges, raspberries, peaches, plums and pippins.

Seville oranges had replaced quinces in the classic English marmalade by the nineteenth century, but Mrs Acworth included only one recipe for orange preserve in her cookery book and did not call it marmalade. The fruits she used most plentifully in preserves were apricots, cherries, pippins and quinces. Toward the end of her life marmalade began to be consumed as a breakfast or tea-time dish, a tradition first established in Scotland. The instructions in her recipes suggest, however, that she usually served them in the traditional manner as a dessert at dinner. She and her husband probably believed that marmalade was an aid to digestion with medicinal properties. They also may have believed, as people did in Tudor and Stuart England, that marmalade was an aphrodisiac.

The recipes we have chosen all produce simple, delicately flavoured preserves. Using modern rules for jam-making, with sterilized jars and a good seal, they will keep well for months. Once opened, they should be stored in the refrigerator.

*TO MAKE JELLY WITH PEECES OF QUINCES IN IT Take
pippins and when they are pared cut them into peeces and boyle them in water
till ye pippins be tender. Then Straine out ye water Cleare from ye pippins and
to Every pint of that Water take a pound of white Sugar and When it is boyl'd
to a surop you having your Quinces ready par boyld, cut them into slices and
tye them up in a Tiffany lawn bagg. Boyle them as quick as you can in the
aforesaid syrop till you think them enough and then in white Marmalade
Dishes put your Jelly and take out ye quinces and lay into it. If you stove it the
jelly will be ye firmer.*

APPLE AND QUINCE JELLY

THIS appetizingly pretty jelly combines the flavours of quince and
apple, which go particularly well together. It is delicious with bread
or toast, or served as an unusual relish with pork or veal.

1 lb (450 g) sweet apples (e.g. Cox's)
about 1 pint (560 ml, 2½ cups) water
1 large or 2 small quinces
1 lb (450 g, 2⅛ cups) preserving sugar

Wash the apples, cut them into quarters and place them in a saucepan
with just enough water to cover them. Bring them to the boil, reduce the
heat and let them simmer for about 10 minutes until they are tender.
Leave them to cool in their water until it is quite cold, before straining it
through a jelly bag. Meanwhile peel, core and slice the quinces and
simmer them in a little water for about 10 minutes, until they begin to
soften. (They will not be as soft as the apples in that time.) Measure
16 fl oz (450 ml, 2 cups or 1 US pint) of the strained apple juice into a
saucepan with the preserving sugar and bring it to the boil. When the
sugar has dissolved, put the quinces in the syrup and, using a sugar
thermometer, leave them boiling at jam temperature (220°F, 105°C) for
about 10 minutes. Test them from time to time and when they have
softened sufficiently and the syrup turns to jelly when spooned on to a
saucer, remove from the heat. Cut the quince slices into small dice with
the edge of a spoon, and pour the jelly with the pieces of quince in it into
clean, warm jam jars. This quantity should make enough to fill two 1 lb
(450 g) jars. Seal them well, and the jelly should keep indefinitely.

MARMALADE OF APRICOCKS Take apricocks. Scald them in faire water. When they begin to feele soft take them out. When you have pilled them slice them thinn. Then take a pound of Apricocks 1 pound of sugar, put to the sugar as much water as will dissolve it then set it on the ffire and boyle it. Then put in your Apricocks and boyle them till they are a little stiff. Then take it up and put it into ½ glasses. Put them into a stove to dry.

APRICOT JAM

'MARMALADE' in Mrs Acworth's vocabulary apparently referred to the consistency rather than the fruit. This recipe makes a good straightforward apricot jam. Mrs Acworth herself probably used it in slices with dessert, as the instruction to dry it in a stove (which we have omitted) suggests a more solid consistency than we would use for spreading on bread or toast.

$1\frac{1}{4}$ lbs (560 g) fresh apricots
1 lb (450 g, $2\frac{1}{8}$ cups) preserving sugar
6 fl oz (170 ml, $\frac{3}{4}$ cup) water

Remove the stones (pits) and roughly chop the apricots. Place them in a pan with just enough water to cover the bottom, bring them to the boil, then let them simmer gently till they are soft but still firm. Bring the sugar to the boil with the rest of the water (about $\frac{1}{4}$ pint, 150 ml, $\frac{1}{2}$ cup) using a sugar thermometer. When the temperature reaches jam height (220°F, 105°C) pour in the apricots and let the whole mixture boil at that temperature for about 10 to 15 minutes. It will be cooked when a little of it spooned on to a saucer begins to set, and wrinkle at the edges. Pour into warmed, clean jars and seal. This quantity will make about enough to fill two 1 lb (450 g) jars.

To PRESERVE CHERRIES Take ye largest Morrello Cherries, gather them while they are pretty ripe before they turne to black. Take off theire stalks. Take theire weight in double refined sugar searced. Then take two or 3 spoonfulls of ye juice of cherries, sugar and all together into the skillet and when your sugar is melted make them boyle as fast as you cann till ye sugar is almost enough. Then put into them half a pint of the jelly of red currants soo let them boyle till they are enough. Put them into a bason and when they are cold into glasses.

CHERRY PRESERVE

SINCE the words jam, marmalade and preserve are used more or less interchangeably nowadays, it is difficult to be sure how much of a distinction Mrs Acworth intended between her preserved cherries and her cherry marmalade; all the more so since she failed to specify what quantity of cherries and sugar called for half a pint of red currant jelly. This recipe produces a rather runny version of jam unless the proportion of red currant jelly, which provides most of the pectin, is very high. It would seem therefore that Mrs Acworth preserved her cherries in a liquid rather than jellied form, for use in pies or sauces. The combination of morello cherries and red currants is used elsewhere in English cookery for sauces to accompany meat.

> 1½ lbs (700 g) morello cherries, not overripe
> 1¼ lbs (560 g, 2¾ cups) preserving sugar
> 8 fl oz (225 ml, 1 cup) red currant jelly

Stone (pit) the cherries, which will then weigh about 1¼ lbs. Put them and any juice that has run out into the saucepan with the sugar, cook over a moderate heat until the sugar has melted, then bring rapidly to the boil, with a sugar thermometer in the pan. As the sugar is approaching jam height (220°F, 105°C) add the red currant jelly, stirring slightly with the thermometer or a metal spoon. Allow to simmer at jam temperature for about 30 minutes, until a little of the liquid spooned out on to a saucer wrinkles slightly and begins to set. Turn off the heat, allow the mixture to cool and then pour it into clean, warmed jars. The quantities given here make enough to fill approximately two 1 lb (450 g) jam jars.

TO MAKE JELLY OF CURRANTS Take your currants when they be ripe, pick of the stalks and bruise them. Take a pint of the Liquor and a pound of the sugar finley beaten, boyle it till it will jelly in the Spoone. Then pour it into your glasses. You may boyle a few currants in your Jelly and lay them in Works.[?] If it Coole in the Glasses stick in the berrys and softly pour in more Jelly upon them.

RED CURRANT JELLY

THIS extremely simple recipe looks very pretty in its jam jars. The whole berries preserved in the jelly are an interesting addition if you are using the jelly as a garnish.

about 2 lbs (900 g) red currants
1 lb (450 g, 2⅛ cups) granulated or preserving sugar

Wash the berries and trim away the stalks. Reserve a few good-looking berries for the decoration. Press the remainder through a sieve, or blend them in a food processor, and measure 16 fl oz (450 ml, 2 cups or 1 US pint) of the liquid into a saucepan. Add the sugar and boil it at jam height (220°F, 105°C) using a sugar thermometer until a little of the mixture spooned on to a saucer turns to jelly (about 10 minutes). Add the whole berries to the mixture and continue boiling for about 1 minute. Allow the jelly to cool slightly, then pour it into sterilized jars and seal well.

TO PRESERVE GRAPES Take grapes when they are Tart Ripe. Before they Turne yellow pill them and Stone them then pour jelly and juice from them as you Cann. Then to a pound of Grapes 3 quarters of a pound of Double Refined Sugar Searced and then let them Stand ½ an hour till the Sugar be melted. Then boyle them soo fast as you Cann till you think they will Jelly and soo put them in your Glasses. For those that you doo not intend to Keepe Long ½ Sugar Will Serve.

GRAPE JAM

IT is likely that Mrs Acworth used white Muscadine grapes in this recipe for they were a variety both available and reliable at the time. This preserve is less sticky and dense than many of her jams. As fashions changed towards the end of her life, she may have served it, in the Scottish style, with toast or cakes as an accompaniment to breakfast or afternoon tea.

1¼ lbs (560 g) white grapes, preferably Muscat
12 oz (340 g, 1⅝ cups) preserving sugar

Peel and seed (pit) the grapes, which will reduce their weight to about 1 lb. Pour the sugar into the saucepan with them (less sugar may be used as Mrs Acworth suggests) and let the mixture stand for half an hour or until the sugar is saturated. Bring to a boil and then allow the jam to simmer at jam height (220°F, 105°C) on a sugar thermometer, for about 40 minutes or until it begins to jelly. When cool pour it into clean jars. The recipe makes about 1 lb (450 g) of jam.

To MAKE JELLY OF PIPPINS Take 10 or 12 large pippins and pare them into a quart of runing water. Boyle them as fast as you can but quarter them and core them first in a pint of water, then straine ye liquor from them and let it stand and settle then leave the bottom. And to a pint of that Liquor take a pound of Double Refined sugar and boyle it as fast as you cann till you find it jelly. As you are a takeing of it of, ring in ye Juice of a Lemon but not lett it boyle with it. Soo put it into glasses. Slice some candied Oranges into your glasses if you please.

PIPPIN JELLY WITH ORANGE

WE have put this recipe with jellies and preserves because it resembles the sort of apple jelly kept in many English store cupboards for eating with bread at tea time. Mrs Acworth equally well may have served it as a dessert dish in little custard glasses, or turned it out of glass jelly moulds. It makes a very pretty dessert. The apple juice turns to an amber colour, which the deeper tone of the pieces of orange complements. The flavour is delicate but quite sweet, and we have used fresh rather than candied oranges to make it less sickly than the original probably was. As for the right sort of apples to use, we have tried Cox's Orange Pippin, which is perhaps the closest in flavour to the pippins available to Mrs Acworth, French Golden Delicious, and some apples sold cryptically as 'cookers'. All worked equally well, each variety producing very slightly different flavours and shades of amber. No doubt commercially produced, unsweetened apple juice could be used as a short cut.

about 3 lbs (just under 1.5 kg) sweet or cooking apples
32 fl oz (900 ml, 4 cups) water
juice of 1 large lemon
1 lb (450 g, 2⅛ cups) granulated sugar
diced oranges

Peel, core and slice the apples into the water in a large saucepan and bring all to the boil together. Allow them to simmer for about 10 minutes, until the apples are tender but not reduced to mush. Add the lemon juice, then strain the liquid through a jelly bag or clean cotton cloth into a bowl. (The logistics of this have to be worked out in advance, unless you are in the habit of straining jellies through jelly bags and already have a hook conveniently placed over a spot in the kitchen or larder, where the cat, dog or baby will not wander.) You should leave the apples straining for at least an hour, and give them a few gentle squeezes to get out the last of the juice before discarding the pulp. Measure 16 fl oz (450 ml, 2 cups or

1 US pint) of juice into a saucepan containing the sugar and bring rapidly to the boil, using a sugar thermometer to measure when it reaches the right temperature for jam (220°F, 105°C). Boil the mixture at this temperature for about 15 minutes, until a little of it spooned on to a saucer turns to jelly. Allow the jelly to cool before pouring it into jars or glasses in which you have put some small dice of orange. Seal the jars if you are planning to keep the jelly as a preserve; refrigerate until you need them if you are serving them for dessert.

To MAKE JELLY OF MUSSEL PLUMBS Put your plumbs into a flagon and the flagon into a kettle of water. Keep them boyling till the juice is quite Clear, then let it run thro a hair seive. Then weigh it and take the weight thereof in Sugar and Put to it. Then boyl them well together till it will Jelly. When it is almost boyl'd you may put in two grains of musk if you Please. Then let it stand till it is Cold and so put it in your Glasses.

PLUM JELLY

AMONG the many varieties of plum available to Mrs Acworth, we have not been able to discover mussel plums and can only assume that like the shellfish they were dark in colour. This recipe produces an attractive red jelly which is best used like jam. Using Victorias, Stanley plums or Marjorie seedlings, which are all available in British shops in the early autumn, a stiff jelly develops after very little boiling.

1½ lbs (675 g) dark plums
8 oz (225 g, just over 1 cup) preserving sugar

Wash the plums and put them in an ovenproof dish without any water. Cover and place in a moderate oven (gas mark 4, 350°F, 180°C) for about 20 minutes, until they have split open and are very tender, and have made a fair quantity of juice. Strain the juice through a fine sieve into a bowl or jug, then weigh it. Plums weighing 1½ lbs (675 g) should produce about 8 oz (225 ml) of juice. Put the preserving sugar in a saucepan and add the juice. Bring the mixture to a rapid boil using a sugar thermometer. When it has reached the right temperature for jam (220°F, 105°C), reduce the heat slightly and let it continue boiling until a little of the liquid spooned on to a saucer turns to jelly. This should take not much more than 10 minutes. Allow the jelly to cool slightly and then pour it into a sterilized 1 lb (450 g) jam jar. Seal well.

TO PRESERVE WHOLE RASBERRYS Take a pound of farest Rasberrys and a pint of yr juice of the other Rasberrys, 2 pounds of Double Refined Sugar Searced. Put one pound of Sugar into your Juice Which Must be let on the fire and When it boyles skim it. Then put on the Rasberrys and all the While they are boyling strew in yr other pound of Searced Sugar and When your Rasberrys are enough and Jelly then put them in your Glasses. Boyle your Rasberrys in a Pitcher as you Doo for Cleare Cakes and then straine of this a pint of Juice.

RASPBERRY JAM

THIS is what is sometimes called a quick preserve, using equal weights of raspberries and sugar. Very straightforward to make, the result is a jam which has an excellent fresh flavour and keeps well.

2 lbs (900 g) fresh raspberries
2 lbs (900 g, 4¼ cups) preserving sugar

Pick out 1 lb (450 g) of the best raspberries and keep them to one side. Stand the remaining 1 lb (450 g) in a heatproof jug or bowl in a saucepan of boiling water, and boil it until the juice runs out of the raspberries. Strain 1 pint (450 ml, 2 cups) of juice from them through a sieve into another saucepan. Add 1 lb (450 g, 2⅛ cups) sugar and bring it to the boil, skimming it as necessary. As it cooks, add in the whole raspberries and the other pound of sugar. Allow several minutes' boiling for the jelly to set and then put it in clean jars. If you wish to serve it in glasses as a dessert, in the style of Mrs Acworth, it goes well with Macaroons or biscuits. The recipe makes about 3 lbs (1.35 kg) of jam.

TO MAKE RED QUINCE MARMALADE Pare & core your Quinces then wey them & to a pound of quince putt a pound of shugar beaten small & a pint of Liquor. Make your Liquor thus: putt pareings & Cores & 3 or 4 quinces cutt in slices into a large presearving pan & boyle them over a slow fier. Cover it Close and Take Care it does not burn to the bottom. Strane of this liquor & then putt in your Shugar & frute & when it is near anufe break or cutt your Quinces into small peaces as you like it. Keep stirring it to prevent it burning to ye bottom & when it is tender & of a good culler take out some into a spoon & when cool if it Jellys it is done anuff. Then putt it into gally potts & when cold tye it downe close.

QUINCE MARMALADE

QUINCE marmalade was a favoured and traditional English sweet-meat in Mrs Acworth's day, long imported from Portugal, Spain and Italy. As Anne Wilson points out in *The Book of Marmalade* it was commonly produced in brick-shaped boxes. Solid, it was sliced into pieces. Good colour, as Mrs Acworth calls for in this recipe, was an important consideration and could be determined by the type of sugar used. This recipe makes a clear amber jelly with the pieces of quince tightly packed but quite distinct within it. It is delectable on toast or may be used as a dessert in the eighteenth-century style.

about 1½ lb (675 g) quinces
about 1 lb (450 g, 2⅛ cups) preserving sugar
about 16 fl oz (450 ml, 2 cups or 1 US pint) water

The quantities given above are only approximate because it is important to weigh the quinces after you have peeled and cored them, and to use the same weight of sugar and the equivalent proportion of liquid. Put the peel and cores in a saucepan, barely cover them with water and bring to the boil. Reduce the heat and simmer them for at least 10 minutes. Strain the liquid into a bowl. Cut the quinces into quarters and put them in a saucepan with the same weight of sugar and quantity of liquid strained from the peel and cores. Bring them rapidly to the boil and keep them boiling at jam height (220°F, 105°C), using a sugar thermometer, for about 30 minutes. By this time the quinces should be soft and a little of the liquid spooned on to a saucer should turn to jelly. If it is not ready, a further 10 minutes' cooking should suffice. Use a knife and fork to cut the quinces into small pieces in the saucepan as the jelly cools, then pour it all into clean, warm jars. These quantities produce about 3 lbs (1.35 kg) of jam.

CHAPTER EIGHT

DRINKS,
SWEETMEATS
AND SUNDRIES

Orange Wine
Lemon Brandy
Glazed Oranges
Dried Apricots
Milk Punch
Shrewsbury Biscuits
Mincemeat for Mince Pies
Cream Pancakes
Ramekins

Glazed Oranges; Marchpane Sweetmeats; Dried Apricots

T HE recipes in this chapter are all for food and drink that might have been consumed at various times of day, outside the setting of a meal. Some, like the mince pies and pancakes, were for serving on special occasions or at particular seasons. The Milk Punch and Lemon Brandy may have been offered to guests after dinner, and the Orange Wine could have been an alternative to tea, taken with a sweetmeat or a slice of cake.

Numerous recipes for drinks could have been included from Mrs Acworth's book. She made mead and cider and various wines from cowslips, apricots, raisins, quinces, and other fruits. Typical of the day, many of her drinks also served as medicines. She requested a recipe for Yarrow tea in a letter to her sister in which she complained of being 'Nott Quite well'. Yarrow was a native hedgerow plant long thought to have healing properties, not least for the piles, which, judging from the note at the bottom of the recipe, is why Mrs Acworth wanted it. Her recipes for 'Waters' included *aqua mirabilis* and spirits of Lavender, which were cordials, laced with brandy, drunk for various complaints. No complete housewife would have been without a recipe for surfeit water, which, when distilled, was a popular drink widely believed, as Mrs Acworth put it, 'to strengthen the stomach'. Hers was made with a long list of ingredients, including poppies and maidenhair fern, soaked in brandy. Her cooking was a temptation to gluttony and perhaps such drinks relieved the symptoms, yet one wonders whether the complaints were not often complicated by the supposed cures as the over-indulgent fell into an alcoholic stupor. The consumption of cordials thinly disguised as medicinal waters was a tribute which vice paid to virtue in an age of excess.

A letter from her sister-in-law Ann Acworth, dated 25 July 1760, is tucked into the recipe book and sheds some light on the family's arrangements for making cordials. With it is a recipe for black cherry water which uses two gallons of brandy to twelve pounds of black cherries. Ann Acworth was unfortunately unable to oblige Margaretta by distilling any of it that year, since she had a gallon left over from the year before, and could not find brandy that she could afford (not surprisingly since the Seven Years War with France, then raging, had a considerable impact on legitimate imports of brandy). Margaretta, then, did not have a still of her own except possibly for a small vessel known as a Limbeck, in which she made her surfeit water. For distilling large quantities, she had to ask friends or relatives to set their stills to work; or she may have called on one of the several brewers and distillers who lived in the neighbourhood.

We have included Shrewsbury biscuits as sweetmeats along with two recipes for candied fruit. All of these could have found their way equally well on to the tea or dinner table, or might have been proffered on their own. The number of candied sweetmeats could have been extended indefinitely, for Mrs Acworth used all sorts of fruit to make little 'cakes' or lozenges which might have filled the place of boiled sweets today. We have included Glazed Oranges and Dried Apricots as only two examples from a great array. The one surprising omission, among so many recipes using ground almonds, is marchpane, now known as marzipan. It is difficult to imagine that the Acworths never ate marchpane, for it was one of the best loved of eighteenth-century sweetmeats. Presumably Mrs Acworth bought it, ready fashioned into fanciful coloured shapes, to add to her own more homely confections.

Ramekins deserve a special mention because this is the only recipe using cheese other than curds in the whole book. English, Welsh and Scottish regional cheeses abounded, and the cheesemongers of London had special arrangements for shipping them in from the provinces. The use of cheese in cooking was also increasing, following Italian and French example. Mrs Acworth, however, did not follow the fashion in this. She may have regarded cheese as a food for the labouring poor, for whom it was a staple. Certainly there was a school of thought that found it vulgar to eat cheese. Perhaps, on the other hand, the Acworths ate their cheese uncooked, with griddle cakes, bread or wigs, and bought it from the local cheesemonger. Ramekins, which in this version were a close relation to Welsh rarebit, make a good appetizer. They may also have been served at the end of a meal as an aid to digestion.

To MAKE ORRINGE WINE Take 6 gallons of Spring water and 12 pound of the Best powdred Sugar and the White of 4 eggs beaten very well. Put them into the water and Sugar and lett them boyle 3 quarters of an Hour. When its cold put in six spoonfulls of ale yeast and 6 ounces of sirrop of cittern or Lemon, well beaten together. Then take the peeles and Juice of 50 orringes, pare your orringes very thinn, and when you begin to pare them take out a Quart or two of ye boyld Water and put in the Parrings as fast as you pare them, that you lose none of ye Spirit of ye orringe Peeles. Then put all together and let it worke two Days and two Nights and put to it two quarts of ye best Renish Wine. Then turn it into a Vessell With ye peeles in it and Stop it very Close and lett it stand a Month or 6 Weeks, or till it is fine enough to bottell and then bottell it. If you intend not to keepe it longe, put in ye Rinds of but 30 orringes, but the other is better. Lett ye Juice of ye orringes be Strained through a Haire sive.

ORANGE WINE

Mrs Acworth used wine abundantly in her cookery. She seems also to have made it in large quantities, for she had a number of recipes for making wine from various fruits. A wine like this one made from oranges might have been offered as a dessert wine. It must have been good if it warranted using 'two quarts of ye best Renish wine' in the making. The version given here has been tried for us by friends, and perhaps only those who are already conversant with some of the mysteries of making wine at home should attempt this recipe, although it produces a pleasant, sweetish wine. (Duncan Gillespie's *Teach Yourself Winemaking and Brewing* (Hodder and Stoughton, 3rd edition, 1985) would be a helpful guide to the uninitiated.)

1 gallon (4.5 litres, 10 US pints) water
32 oz (900 g, 5 cups) granulated sugar
1 stiffly beaten egg white
18 fl oz (500 ml, 2¼ US cups) yeast-based starter
8 oranges
1 fl oz (30 ml, 1 tablespoon) concentrated lemon juice
12 fl oz (340 ml, 1½ cups) medium-dry white wine, e.g. hock

Boil the water, sugar and egg white together for ¾ hour. Allow it to cool, then add the starter, the juice of the oranges, their thinly pared rind (leaving out as much as possible of the white pith, which is bitter) and the concentrated lemon juice. Leave this mixture in a well-covered crock for 2 or 3 days. Then add the white wine, cover it well again and leave it for 4 to 6 weeks. During this period the wine can be racked, or siphoned, to remove the sediment and the quantity of liquid can then be made up with boiled water which has been allowed to cool, or with a light syrup. When the wine is crystal-clear and you can be sure that fermentation has ceased, pour it into sterilized bottles and cork it well. We would recommend keeping it for several months before drinking.

To make Lemon Brandy Paire the Rinds of Seven Lemons thinn then put to em a quart of Brandy and Let it Steep 48 Hours. Then boyle a pint of Water With ½ a pound of fine Sugar till its Cleane Scum'd. So put it Scalding Hott to yr peells and brandy and let it stand Close Coverd 24 Hours then Straine it and boyle it up. The brandy I like is Done in all Receipts as this receipt only I put a quart of Water and 3 quarters of a pound of Sugar and let it Run through a Jelly Bagg.

LEMON BRANDY

This recipe makes a good punch, which can be drunk hot or cold. To make the brandy go further the alternative version given in the recipe may be preferred. The following list of ingredients is for the first version.

7 lemons
1 pint plus 12 fl oz (900 ml, 1 US quart) brandy
16 fl oz (450 ml, 1 US pint) uncarbonated mineral water
8 oz (225 g, just over 1 cup) caster or granulated sugar

Pare the peels of the 7 lemons and add them to the brandy. Let this stand for 2 days. Then boil your mixture of mineral water and sugar and add it hot to the brandy and peel. (The full quantity of sugar makes rather a sweet drink, for our taste.) Cover it and after 24 hours strain the peel out, boil the remaining punch and put into your bowl or, if you wish to keep it, a sterilized bottle.

TO GLAZE ORANGES Take the finest China oranges you can get, Peel them & Part the Cloves but do not let out any of the juice. Let them lay all Night to dry. Next day boyl some double refined Sugar to a Candy height & then Dip in the Cloves one by one & dry them on a peice of Glass. They are very Pretty for a Desart.

GLAZED ORANGES

As Mrs Acworth remarks, this is a very pretty dessert, best served in a glass dish with chips of the hardened caramel.

2 or 3 oranges
3 oz (85 g, ½ cup) caster sugar
1 tablespoon water

Peel the oranges and remove all the pith from the outside. Separate the segments and leave them on a plate to dry for 7 or 8 hours, or overnight. Bring the sugar, just moistened with the water, boiling to hard ball temperature (250°F, 120°C) on the sugar thermometer. Lower the heat while you dip the segments into the caramel using skewers to avoid burning your fingertips, returning it to the boil once or twice to keep it from setting. Lay the orange segments on a plate or a piece of glass and serve them when the caramel has set.

TO DRY APRICOCKS Gather them before they're too ripe, pare them as thin as you can and stone and weigh ym. To every pound of fruit take half a pound of Double refined Sugar finely beaten and sifted, melt it with a little fair water and with your apricocks set it over the fire and let it Boyl till the fruit begins to look clear and you think ym more than helf enough preserv'd. Let ym stand in the syrup all night. Next day lay ym on glasses to Dry in your stove. It ye best way to Dry ym in halves. This way you may do the Chips in with them. They look very pretty.

DRIED APRICOTS

GIVEN the ready availability of dried apricots in the shops, there seemed little reason beyond curiosity to try out this particular recipe, except that Mrs Acworth said they looked pretty, and therefore meant them presumably to add colour to a dish of dried or candied fruit among her desserts. In fact this recipe, along with her others for dried fruits, rewards perseverance. The end result is mid-way between what we would recognize as dried fruit and the rich glacé fruits of Christmas time. This is one of the few recipes for which an eighteenth-century kitchen would have been altogether more trouble-saving than a modern one, for it undoubtedly would have had a suitable warm place in which to leave the apricots to dry for as long as they took.

1½ lbs (675 g) fresh apricots
10 oz (280 g, 1¾ cups) caster sugar
4 fl oz (115 g, ½ cup) water

Place the halved, stoned (pitted) (but not necessarily peeled) apricots, sugar and water together in a saucepan and bring all together to the boil, using a sugar thermometer to measure when they reach soft ball temperature (240°F, 115°C). Boil them for no more than 5 minutes, when the fruit should feel soft but still firm. Leave the apricots standing in the syrup overnight, then arrange them carefully, not overlapping, on a piece of lightly oiled or buttered greaseproof (waxed) paper, spooning a little of the syrup over each apricot. Place the apricots on their paper over a large flat sieve or, if you have not got one, a plate, and put it in the oven at its lowest possible heat. Leave the door of the oven ajar, and let the apricots dry for as long as you can. They may be taken out whenever you need to use the oven for something else or overnight, and replaced again as many times as necessary, until the syrup has hardened to crystals and the fruit itself is dried.

MILK PUNCH Take four larg fair Lemons, pare off the Rinds as thin as possible and put them to a Quart of the best French Brandy; let them steep two or three Hours, then take them all out and put in the juice of the Lemons strain'd from the Pulp, with two Quarts of Spring Water that has been Boil'd and stood till cold, and something less than a pound of double refin'd Sugar. Mix them well together and when the Sugar is quite disolvd add a Pint of Milk boiling hot. Cover it up close till the next Morning, then pass it thro' a Dimity Jelly Bag till it is perfectly clear. Let there be a good deel of the Curd in the Bag which will make it drop fine very soon. Put it into clean dry Bottles, cork it close & set them in a cool place. It will keep two or three Months. This receipt was given me by a Lady who was Excelent at Makeing this sort of Liquor.

MILK PUNCH

THIS simple recipe makes a good punch which keeps for several weeks and can be offered as an unusual drink for Christmas or special occasions. Milk punch, in which milk replaced wine, became fashionable in the early eighteenth century. Like other punches, it was served in a bowl, usually with biscuits or toast floating on it.

4 large lemons
1 pint plus 12 fl oz (900 ml, 1 US quart) brandy
same quantity of uncarbonated mineral water
12 oz (340 g, 2 cups) caster or granulated sugar
16 fl oz (450 ml, 1 US pint) milk

Squeeze the lemons and keep the juice. Grate or pare the zest into a bowl and pour the brandy over it. Leave it to stand for 2 or 3 hours, strain the brandy into another bowl, strain the lemon juice over it and add the water and sugar. Stir them well and add the boiling milk, which will curdle straight away. Cover the bowl and leave it overnight. Strain the mixture through a jelly bag. The mixture should run clear on first straining, leaving a curd in the bag. Scald 4 standard-sized wine bottles with boiling water, then pour in the punch and cork the bottles.

SHREWSBURY CAKES Take a pound & quarter of flower, 3 quarters of a pound of Butter or More, half a pound of sugar. Wet it with a small glass of Brandy 2 eggs leaving out the whites, a little rose water. Cut them out with the top of a wine glass.

SHREWSBURY BISCUITS

HERE is a recipe that has survived in recognizable form from at least the late seventeenth century to the present day. Mrs Acworth kept two recipes in her book, one sent by a friend who used nutmeg and cinnamon, and this one written out in her own hand. Numerous other versions are to be found. Florence White's *Good Things in England* quotes a recipe using nutmeg, caraway seeds and sack from the cookery book of a Shrewsbury family dated between 1630 and 1750. Jane Grigson in *British Cookery* quotes the proverb 'as short as a Shrewsbury cake' dating back to 1700 and gives an early recipe with caraway and coriander seeds. From the other side of the Atlantic, an Annapolis recipe book of 1811, quoted in the compendium *Maryland's Way*, offers Shrewsbury cakes made with currants, nutmeg and brandy. We have childhood memories of Shrewsbury biscuits with a heart-shaped hole cut out of half of the biscuits. The ones with holes in would then be sandwiched to the others with strawberry jam.

10 oz (280 g, 2 cups) flour
3 oz (85 g, $\frac{1}{4}$ cup plus 1 tablespoon) each of butter and margarine
4 oz (115 g, $\frac{5}{8}$ cup) granulated or caster sugar
1 egg yolk
about 2 fl oz (60 g, $\frac{1}{4}$ cup) brandy
1 tablespoon rose-water

Sift the flour into a mixing bowl and add the butter and margarine cut into small pieces. Work them together with your hands as if for pastry, until they are well mixed into a consistency like breadcrumbs. Stir in first the sugar, then the egg yolk mixed with the brandy and rose-water. Knead the dough to a moist pastry. You may wish to leave it in the refrigerator for 15 minutes to become firm before rolling it out about $\frac{1}{2}$ inch (1 cm) thick on a floured board. Cut the dough into shapes and bake at gas mark 4 (350°F, 180°C) for about 30 minutes, until they are golden brown.

THE RECEIPT OF THE MINCE PYES THAT MY DEAR MAMMA ALLWAYS MADE & WAS GENERALLY ADMIRED 4 pounds & a half of Egs boyld. hard & chopd. fine, 3 pounds of beef sewet shreed & chopd. fine, two pounds of appels shopd. as the above, 3 pounds of currants washd. & made very dry, 2 pounds of reasons of the sun stoned & chopd., 3 pounds of Lisbon shugar, Nutmegs, Mace and Cloves one ounce each beat to a powder. Candied Citirn, Orange & Lemmon peal, one ounce each, these to be cut into thin slices. You may putt in more of the sweetmeats if you like it. Mix all this up together with your hands very well & putt it into a pan & letting it stand in a cool dry place tyd. downe it will keep a Quarter of a Year. I have keepd. it so Long & it has been Very Good.

MINCEMEAT FOR MINCE PIES

THIS is a very good recipe for mincemeat, close to modern recipes in flavour despite the unusual addition of hard-boiled eggs. It makes deliciously spicy mince pies.

8 small eggs, weighing 1 lb 2 oz (500 g) uncooked
5 oz (140 g, 2½ cups) each of fresh breadcrumbs and shredded suet
(kidney fat)
1 large cooking apple, weighing 10 oz (280 g) unpeeled
12 oz (340 g, 3 cups) currants
8 oz (225 g, 2 cups) raisins
10 oz (280 g, 1¾ cups) dark brown sugar
1 tablespoon each ground nutmeg and mace
1 teaspoon ground cloves
2 oz (60 g, ½ cup) chopped mixed candied peel

Boil the eggs hard, cool them and shred them using a food processor or cheese grater. Mix them with the breadcrumbs and suet. Peel, quarter and core the apple and shred it too. Mix it into the breadcrumbs and suet, then add all the remaining ingredients. Stir well and put it into sterilized jars. Seal well and keep in a cool, dark cupboard. Mrs Acworth's recipe for the pastry for mince pies is on p. 125.

CREAM PANCAKES One pint of Cream, 3 Spoonfulls of Flower, 6 Eggs Whites, & all Half a pound of Butter, a Little Sugar. They will fry Themselves, Viz they will Want no additions of Butter to fry them.

CREAM PANCAKES

PANCAKES were associated with Shrove Tuesday, the day before the beginning of Lent, which was known then, as it is now, as Pancake Day. By Mrs Acworth's time they were usually made with milk or cream rather than water and sometimes enriched with spices, sherry or brandy. They would have been fried over the open fire using a long-handled copper pan. This recipe is less extravagant than many contemporary ones for pancakes but it is still rich, and delicious. Serve the pancakes rolled up with lemon juice and sugar or with jam, as a treat for breakfast, or with more elaborate sauces as a dessert for dinner.

5 egg whites
3 oz (85 g, ⅔ cup) flour
1 oz (30 g, 2 tablespoons) granulated sugar
8 oz (225 g, 1 cup) butter
16 fl oz (450 ml, 2 cups or 1 US pint) thin or thick cream

Beat the egg whites stiff and whisk in flour and sugar. Melt the butter and add it and the cream, beating well with a whisk. As Mrs Acworth remarks you will not need any additional butter to fry the pancakes. This quantity will make about a dozen thin pancakes.

To MAKE RAMAKINS Pat your Cheese either Cheshire or Glocestershire, put it in and beet it in a stone Mortar. Beat it soft then put in the yolk of an egg and a little pepper. Beat it again till it comes up Clear from the pestle. Cut little square bits of bread pretty thick, spread ye Cheese thick on ym yn put ym in a frying pan with a bit of butter the quantity of a patt. Fry them very slow till the bread is brown. Hold them a good while before the fire. Brown the top with a Sallimander.

RAMEKINS

THE word 'ramekins' derives from a Flemish recipe for bread and cheese, though English cooks very probably made this simple dish on their own initiative, giving it this name later. At some point, a variation of the dish developed using breadcrumbs and the whites as well as the yolks of eggs. This was cooked in little dishes which in turn came to be called ramekins, and was like a small cheese soufflé. Mrs Acworth's recipe was given her by a friend, along with recipes 'To keep Asparagrass all year', 'To dry cherrys without Sugar' and Mr Andrews's recipe for a ham pie. The salamander mentioned in the recipe would have been a hot iron, laid across the cooked cheese to score it with brown lines; a substitute for the modern grill (broiler). As a tasty variation on the traditional 'Welsh rarebit' they make a satisfying snack. Served in small pieces as her friend suggested, they are a good appetizer to serve with an aperitif.

8 oz (225 g, about 2 cups) grated Cheshire or Double Gloucester
cheese (a well-flavoured Cheddar does well, too)
1 egg yolk
freshly ground pepper, to taste
about 2 oz (60 g, ¼ cup) butter
4 slices of bread from a large loaf

Grate the cheese then mix in the egg yolk and pepper. If you are using a food processor, use the grating attachment, then blend until the mixture forms a smooth ball. Spread it on to the bread, heat the butter in a frying pan until it froths, then fry each slice whole for about 5 minutes, finishing it off under the grill (broiler) so that it browns slightly. Cut up the slices into bite-sized squares after cooking, because otherwise the cheese runs into the pan and becomes rather uncontrollable. Serve straight away, or keep hot in the oven.

BIBLIOGRAPHY

The following are the main written sources on which we have relied in compiling this edition. We are particularly indebted to the works of the twentieth-century cookery writers cited here for much indispensable guidance in reconstructing Margaretta Acworth's recipes.

Manuscripts

C 107/108, cookery book of Margaretta Acworth, Public Record Office, Chancery Masters' Exhibits, Case of Ommaney vs. Butcher.
PROB 11/670, 11/1076, 11/1607, Public Record Office, Prerogative Court of Canterbury, Wills and Administrations of A. R. Buckeridge, Abraham Acworth, and Buckeridge Ball Acworth.
Rate Books of St John the Evangelist Parish, Westminster, 1745–94, Westminster City Library Archives Department.

Published Sources

Ayrton, Elisabeth, *The Cookery of England* (London, 1974).
Bannerman, W. Bruce, ed., *Miscellanea Genealogica et Heraldica*, vol. iii, 4th Series (London, 1910).
Beard, James, *American Cookery* (Boston, 1972).
Berriedale-Johnson, Michelle, *Olde English Recipes* (Loughton, 1981).
Black, Maggie, *A Heritage of British Cooking* (London, 1978).
Carter, Charles, *The Complete Practical Cook* (London, 1730), reprinted by Prospect Books (London, 1984).
David, Elizabeth, *English Bread and Yeast Cookery* (London, 1977).
  Spices, Salt and Aromatics in the English Kitchen (London, 1970).
Drummond, Sir Jack C. and Anne Wilbraham, *The Englishman's Food* (London, 1939).
Gentleman's Magazine, 1745–81.
General Advertiser, 1745.
Fitzgibbon, Theodora, *The Food of the Western World* (London, 1976).
Glasse, Hannah, *The Art of Cookery made Plain and Easy* (London, 1747), reprinted by Prospect Books with a glossary by Alan Davidson (London, 1983).
Greene, W. A., *Pedigree of Acworth of Bedfordshire* (London, 1910).
Grigson, Jane, *Fruit Book* (London, 1982).
  Vegetable Book (London, 1978).
  British Cookery. The Observer Guide to Food From Britain (London, 1984).

Hammond-Harwood House Association, *Maryland's Way. The Hammond-Harwood House Cook Book* (Annapolis, 1963).

Hartley, Dorothy, *Food in Britain* (London, 1954).

Kidder, Edward, *E. Kidder's Receipts of Pastry and Cookery for the Use of his Scholars* (London, 1720?).

Maclean, Virginia, *A Short-Title Catalogue of Household and Cookery Books published in the English Tongue 1701–1800* (London, 1980).

Mennell, Stephen, *All Manner of Food: Eating and Taste in England and France from the Middle Ages to the Present* (Oxford and New York, 1985).

Nott, John, *The Cook's and Confectioner's Dictionary: or, the Accomplish'd Housewife's Companion* (London, 1723), reprinted by Lawrence Rivington with a glossary by Elizabeth David (London, 1980).

Parker, Audrey, *A Country Recipe Notebook* (London, 1979).

Peckham, Ann, *The Complete English Cook; or Prudent Housewife* (Leeds, 1767).

Petits Propos Culinaires (London, three times a year since 1979).

Raffald, Elizabeth, *The Experienced English Housekeeper* (Manchester, 1769), reprinted by E. and W. Books Ltd (1970) and Redwood Press for Paul Minet reprints (1972).

Scurfield, George and Cecilia, *Home Baked* (London, 1956).

Smith, Alice, 'The John Trot Fault: An English Dinner Table in the 1750s', *Petits Propos Culinaires* 15 (London, 1983).

Smith, Eliza, *The Compleat Housewife* (London, 1727), reprinted by Literary Services and Production Ltd (London, 1968).

Smith, Michael, *Fine English Cookery* (London, 1973).

Stead, Jennifer, *Food and Cooking in 18th Century Britain: History and Recipes* (English Heritage, 1985).

Trusler, John, *The Honours of the Table, or, Rules for Behaviour during Meals* (London, 1788).

Westminster Poll Books, 1749, 1770 and 1780, University of London, Institute of Historical Research.

White, Florence, *Good Things in England: A Practical Cookery Book for everyday use, containing Traditional and Regional Recipes suited to Modern Tastes* (London, 1932).

Wilson, C. Anne, *The Book of Marmalade: Its Antecedents, Its History and Its Role in the World Today* (London, 1985).
Food and Drink in Britain (London, 1973).

Young, Arthur, *Travels in France during the years 1787, 1788, 1789* (London, 1792).

INDEX

Page numbers in *italics* refer to illustrations